NO-FAIL ART

PROJECTS

·Arliss Burchard·

No-Fail Art Projects

100 SUCCESS-ORIENTED LESSONS FOR THE PRIMARY GRADES

PARKER PUBLISHING COMPANY
West Nyack, New York 10995

© 1990 by
PARKER PUBLISHING COMPANY

West Nyack, N.Y.

10   9   8   7   6   5   4   3   2   1

Library of Congress Cataloging-in-Publication Data

Burchard, Arliss, 1924–
   No-fail art projects : 100 success-oriented lessons for the primary
grades / Arliss Burchard.
       p.   cm.
    ISBN 0-13-622481-4
    1. Art—Study and teaching (Primary)—United States.   2. Creative
activities and seat work.   I. Title.
N361.B85   1990   90-30782
372.5′044—dc20   CIP

ISBN   0-13-622481-4

PARKER PUBLISHING COMPANY
BUSINESS & PROFESSIONAL DIVISION
A division of Simon & Schuster
West Nyack, New York 10995

Printed in the United States of America

ABOUT THE AUTHOR

Arliss Burchard received an A.A. degree from Metropolitan State College in Denver, after which she earned a B.A. in speech pathology from the University of Northern Colorado. Her teaching certificate was granted the following year from the University of Colorado at Denver. She earned an M.A. in learning disabilities at the University of Colorado at Boulder.

Mrs. Burchard was a resource room teacher with the Denver public schools for twelve years before retiring.

Children in grades 1 through 6 look forward to art class and the opportunity to see their skills on display in the classroom. The most important consideration for the teacher in planning the lesson is the success of the finished product.

Although the original ideas for these projects came about while teaching children with learning disabilities, *all* children need to learn how to use basic skills involving audio and visual perception as well as motor skills. The projects in *No-Fail Art Projects* were developed to incorporate these skills in a success-oriented format using art ideas. Many of the lessons can be used as part of a whole learning program, or as reinforcement in various subject areas. In our busy, pressure-filled society, we sometimes overlook that most children need many repetitions to learn basic skills such as cutting, tracing, and fitting pieces together. Individual creativity comes easily after the various components have been mastered.

Art projects provide an ideal situation in which to teach listening—a necessity in following directions in any learning situation. They can also be a painless way of learning to organize materials and time; a chance to practice sequencing and joining parts to a whole. These are valuable assets that can transfer to other classroom situations or to the child's general environment. Any time a child feels success in an attempt, he or she gains more of the self-confidence that helps the child build rapport with his or her peers. Rapport with peers can make the difference between a child who is willing to try something new, including cooperation, and one who becomes a potential behavior problem because of his or her basic inadequacy.

You will see that many of the project objectives are repetitive, and that is as it should be if we are aiming for success. These projects are concerned with the basic needs for learning: auditory perception in following directions, listening (not just hearing), sequencing, figure-ground, visual perception, motor activity, and success of an end product that can be shown with pride. Incidental to these learning experiences are other concepts and ideas such as vocabulary, color coordination, appropriate use of size for visual harmony, reading directions, using measurement, and other math-related concepts.

The format for *No-Fail Art Projects* has been chosen with ease of use in mind. It is not intended to be used as a reference but rather as a teacher's guide that can help a classroom aide in assembling supplies and materials. The supplies are the usual "hardware" found in the classroom. Materials have been limited to the kinds of paper and other items readily available, even on limited budgets. However, feel free to substitute other materials that are available to you. For instance, there are many kinds of glue and adhesives on the market, and if you have a preference, by all means use what you like.

The objectives are listed first so that any special need may be detected quickly. The remainder of the information is listed in the order necessary to carry out the project. Notes and variations are included where they might be helpful.

Readers interested in needlework will recognize some ideas adapted from various forms of this craft. Needlepoint and cross stitch lend themselves to pictures that require counting and careful visual sequencing as well as figure-ground. Quilt patterns can be used successfully in figure-ground and in matching. Their construction requires motor control, and can be used to teach math skills. This is a good time to help a child see that perfection is not a requirement. Bits can be snipped here and there to achieve a better "fit." Be ready at all times to help in making adjustments, thereby defusing frustration and showing that corrections can be made in any situation. Children need to learn that making mistakes is not always a lack of success. When geometric patterns are too difficult, another needlework idea can be used. Appliqué or overlay techniques can be used instead of exact matching.

Seasonal and other pictures from the media can often be adapted to a paper project. By pointing out the source of some of your own ideas, children can be encourage to be watchers for new project ideas, a change from the usual current events assignments.

Wherever possible, full-size patterns have been included and can be used to make thermofax copies or patterns from cardboard.

I hope that *No-Fail Art Projects* will encourage not only children, but will reassure teachers that art work or paper projects are not just busy work. Art is an important part of the education of children and should not be used to fill bulletin boards, to please the principal, or to fill in odd times in a day's schedule. Children need hands-on activities to encourage development of physical as well as creative abilities. In this respect, children can always succeed!

Arliss Burchard

Objectives have been included so that you may coordinate the projects into a regular curriculum and meet the requirement for management through these objectives.

The projects are arranged alphabetically in the order of the fall-to-spring school year. With some adaptations, many of the lessons can be used at any time of the year.

For ease of operation and to save time, it is necessary to have basic supplies on hand at all times. These include:

pencils	scissors
needles	glue, paste, or other adhesive
clear tape	lightweight string
erasers	rulers
thread	stapler
circle patterns or compass	hole puncher
paper cutter	

The following materials should also be kept on hand:

posterboard	tissue paper
drawing paper	newsprint
old newspapers	gift wrap
construction paper	wallpaper
tablet cardboard backs	cardboard tubes (from paper products)
acetate sheets	

Each project lists the specific items needed. In most cases, paper sizes are included, but paper stock size varies, so you may have to adjust according to the situation. Cutting the paper helps to teach conservation and reduces the frustration some children experience because of perceptual or organizational problems.

All directions are given step by step. This is important if you are to achieve the no fail results, and it exerts the control many children need. Those who rush and regret will learn to stay with the group. At the same time, the procrastinator will be nudged to keep up. Best of all, children who have difficulty listening and/or following directions will be integrated into the group. The patterns are included with the directions and can be copied onto heavy stock for tracing.

Alternatives or extra ideas for use are given at the end of some of the projects to help you extend the possibilities according to your needs. However, adapt your own ideas into the lessons, for each group of children has its own character, and only you know best how to meet the children's needs.

CONTENTS

AUTUMN

WINTER

SPRING

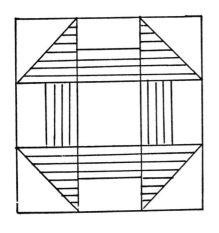

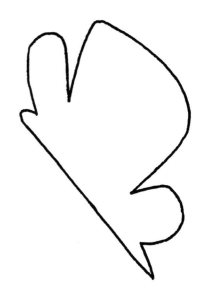

❖❖ **ANYTIME ACTIVITIES** ❖❖

BUTTERFLY MURAL

Objectives: • Following directions for a common goal
• Figure-ground and parts-to-a-whole understanding
• Fine motor control

Supplies: Pencils
Scissors
Glue
Crayons if paper is not used for details

Materials: Poster or construction paper 9″ × 12″ for background for each section of the mural. One combination of colors might be copper, orange, pink, and yellow. Any group of four colors may be used. Paper for butterflies and flowers must be in harmony, and size depends on the size of pattern used. You will also need small pieces of contrasting paper for details and patterns for butterflies and flowers.

Directions:

1. Explain that each child will be making one section of the mural. If possible, let children choose colors and patterns they would like to use. However, there should be no two alike.

2. Distribute the supplies and materials and begin the tracing and cutting.

3. Add details by using crayons or by cutting them from paper and gluing them in place.

4. When all pieces for each section have been made, arrange them on the background to be sure the total effect is pleasing.

5. Glue the pieces in place.

6. When all sections are completed, tack them up on a display board.

Note: Each section of the mural will look best if it is not crowded. For instance, a large butterfly should not have anything else with it. A large flower might have a very small butterfly near the center of the flower. Smaller butterflies or flowers may be grouped together loosely.

BUTTERFLY MURAL

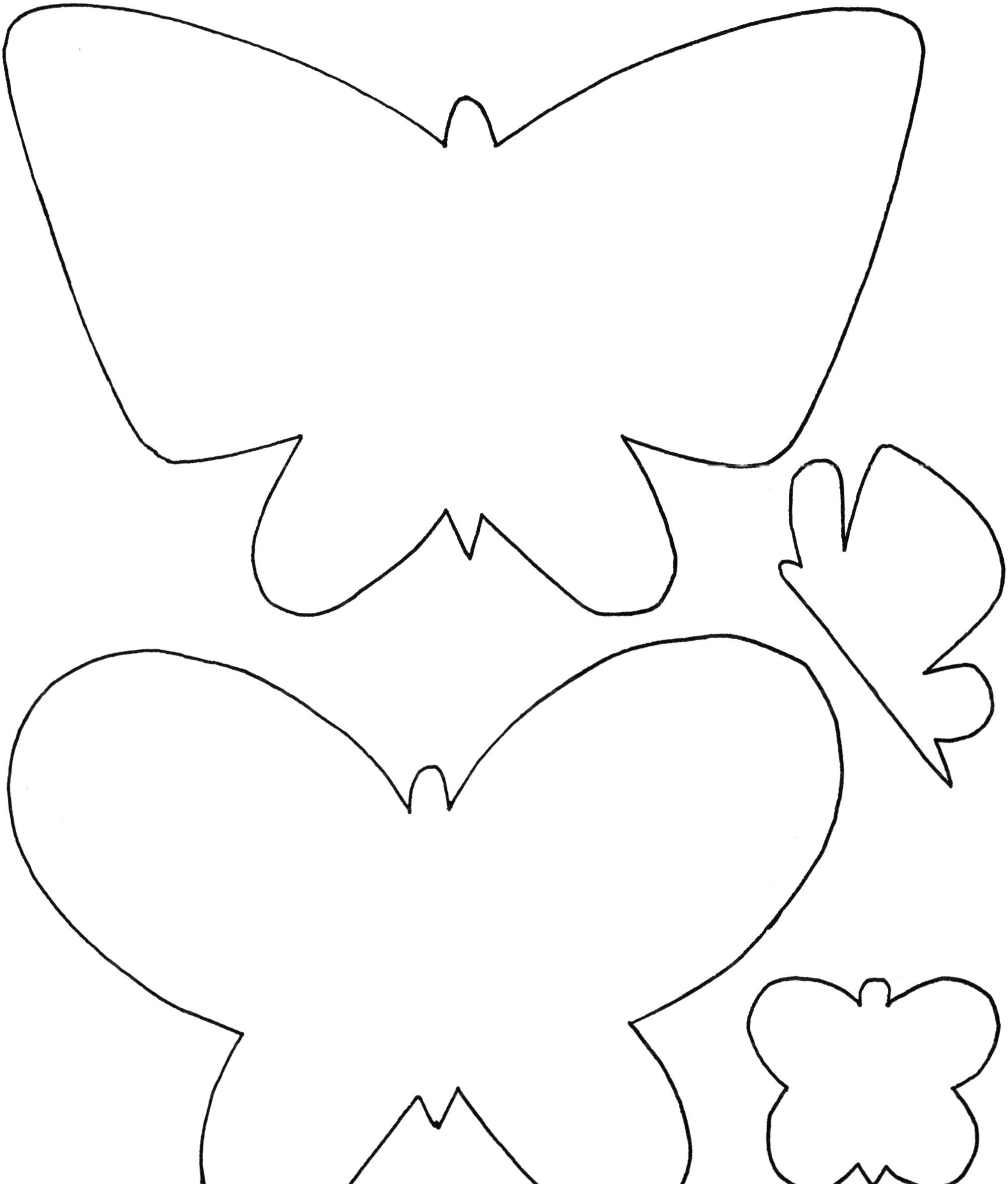

BUTTERFLY MURAL

——— CANDLES ———

Objectives: • Measurement practice
              • Visual discrimination
              • Following directions

Supplies: Rulers
            Pencils
            Scissors
            Glue

Materials: Paper tubes (towels, toilet paper, etc.)
            Paper (color to suit use, size determined by the length of the tube)
            Two-inch squares of yellow tissue paper

Directions:

1. If it is necessary to cut the tubes for proper length, the teacher should do this ahead of time.

2. Distribute supplies and materials; paper aside.

3. Place the tube end on the paper and trace around it. Measure about 1/2″ out from this circle and draw a second circle for a cutting line.

4. Cut out the circle, and then using it as a pattern, cut out a second circle.

5. Clip the circles from the edge to the inner line at 1/2″ intervals and fold toward the center, but do not crease too hard.

6. Place the circles of paper on the ends of the tube and glue the tabs to the sides of the tube.

7. Measure the length of the tube and write down the measurement.

8. Measure the paper (either scrap paper or the paper to cover the tube) to the length written down, in several places, and draw a line so the paper can be cut to the proper size.

9. Wrap the paper around the tube, overlapping it about 1/2″.

10. Measure, mark, and cut so that the paper will be straight. Lay the paper aside.

11. Place glue on one end of the rectangle of paper and fasten it to the tube. Then roll the tube on the paper and glue the other end over the first.

12. Press the square of tissue paper over the flat end of a pencil, apply a dab of glue, and press it to the center of one end of the tube.

Note: For younger children, it might be easier to have them trace a circle pattern. Also, the paper for the candle could be cut to size instead of measured and then cut.
The candles may be glued to a heavy piece of cardboard that has been covered with appropriate paper. The candles can be made very festive by using a metallic paper or by drawing or using cut-out designs or by adding a greeting such as "Happy Birthday."

CAT OR LION

Objectives:
- Fine motor control
- Recognition of parts to the whole
- Visual motor integration

Supplies:
Scissors
Glue
Rulers, if measuring and cutting pieces
Stapler (optional)

Materials: Poster or construction paper, color of your choice. One strip $1\frac{1}{2}'' \times 12''$ for body. One strip $1/2''$ to $3/4'' \times 6\frac{1}{2}''$ for head of cat. Increase width to $1''$ for the lion. Quarter-inch strips, various lengths, for other parts.

Directions:

1. Discuss the various members of the cat family, how they are alike, and how they are different.

2. Distribute supplies and materials.

3. Using the wide, long strip, overlap the ends about $1/2''$ and glue them to form a circle.

4. Crease about $1\frac{1}{2}''$ on either side of the glued end. Either glue or staple about $1/2''$ from the crease.

5. Cut out a V shape in the center of the strip where it was glued or stapled. This forms the feet.

6. Using the strip for the head, form it into a circle, overlap the ends about $1/2''$, glue. Then glue to the top of the wide strip opposite the feet.

7. Using the narrow strips, make small circles and glue them inside the head circle for the eyes and mouth.

8. Pinch two small circles into triangles and glue them to the top of the head.

9. Glue another narrow strip in place for a tail.

10. For the lion, using the wider head strip, fringe one edge for the lion's mane.

11. Also, the tail of the lion should be fringed on the end.

staples

CIRCUS WAGONS AND ANIMALS

Objectives: • Classification of animals
• Eye-hand coordination
• Figure-ground identification

Supplies: Pencils
Scissors
Glue
Fine-tip felt pens (optional)

Materials: Construction paper 9″ × 12″, for two wagons
Poster or construction paper (colors and amounts appropriate for the animal used)
Construction paper if backgrounds are to be used
Patterns

Directions:

1. Discuss the circus and what kinds of animals one would see there. Point out that some animals seen in a zoo or on a farm would not be seen in a circus. Also talk about why most animals in a circus parade would be in cages.

2. Distribute supplies and materials. Trace and cut out those patterns to be used. Perhaps each child could make one animal rather than all of them.

3. Using pencils or felt-tip pens, draw in the features of the animals and stripes on the tiger.

4. Arrange the animals behind the bars of the cages, letting some parts come in front of the bars as if the animal is reaching out. This would give the display more depth. Glue in place.

5. Place the horses in front of the wagons.

6. Arrange the wagons in a row along the bulletin board, or mount them on a background for individual pictures.

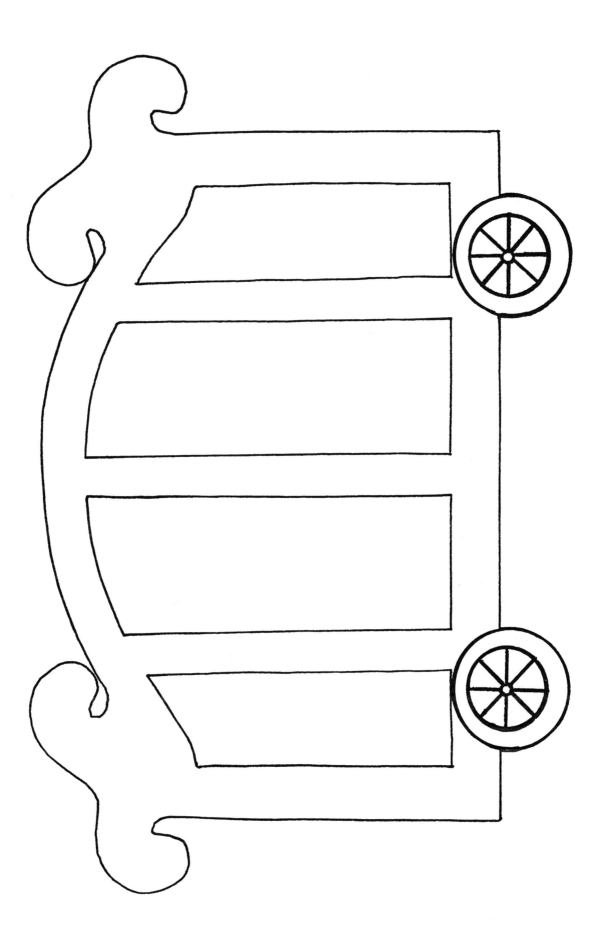

CIRCUS ANIMALS

———— CLOWN CALENDAR ————

Objectives: • Sequencing
• Following directions
• Learning names of days and months
• Visual and motor control

Supplies: Pencils
Scissors
Glue
Paper fasteners

Materials: Construction paper, 9″ × 12″, orange
Construction or poster paper, 6″ × 8″, tan
Construction paper, 4″ × 9″, any color
Poster paper, 3″ × 6″, white
Small pieces of red and black poster paper
One sheet of tagboard with duplicated circles
Patterns

Directions:

1. In discussion, determine the children's knowledge of the names of the days of the week and months of the year.

2. Distribute materials and patterns.

3. Using the orange paper, trace and cut out the clown head and eyebrows. Set aside all pieces.

4. Using the tan paper, trace and cut out the face.

5. Trace and cut out the neck ruffle.

6. Using the white paper, trace and cut out the mouth and eyeballs.

7. Using the black paper, trace and cut out the pupils of the eyes.

8. Using the shape and cut-outs as a guide, glue the face onto the head.

9. Glue the neck ruffle onto the back of the head, making sure the holes are matched.

10. Glue the facial features in place, being careful to match the spots where the paper fasteners will be pushed through.

11. Cut out the circles. Punch a hole with a heavy needle where the paper fastener will go through.

12. Place the circle with the name of the months on the back of the head on the left side, and fasten.

13. Place the circle with the names of the days on the back of the head on the right side, and fasten.

14. Place the large circle with the numbers on the back of the head, and fasten.

15. To set the date, reach behind the head and turn the circles to the correct month, day, and date.

CLOWN CALENDAR

CLOWN CAL

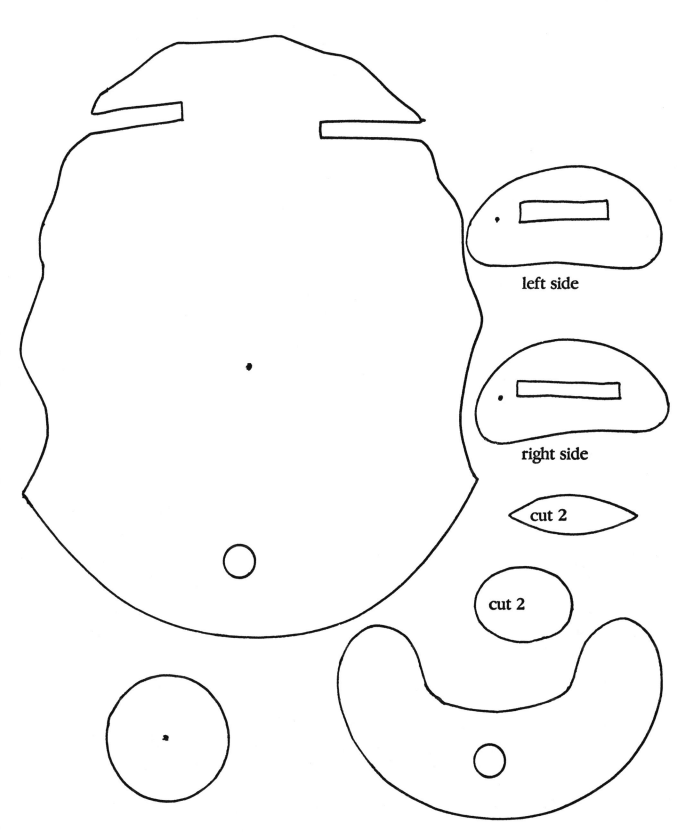

left side

right side

cut 2

cut 2

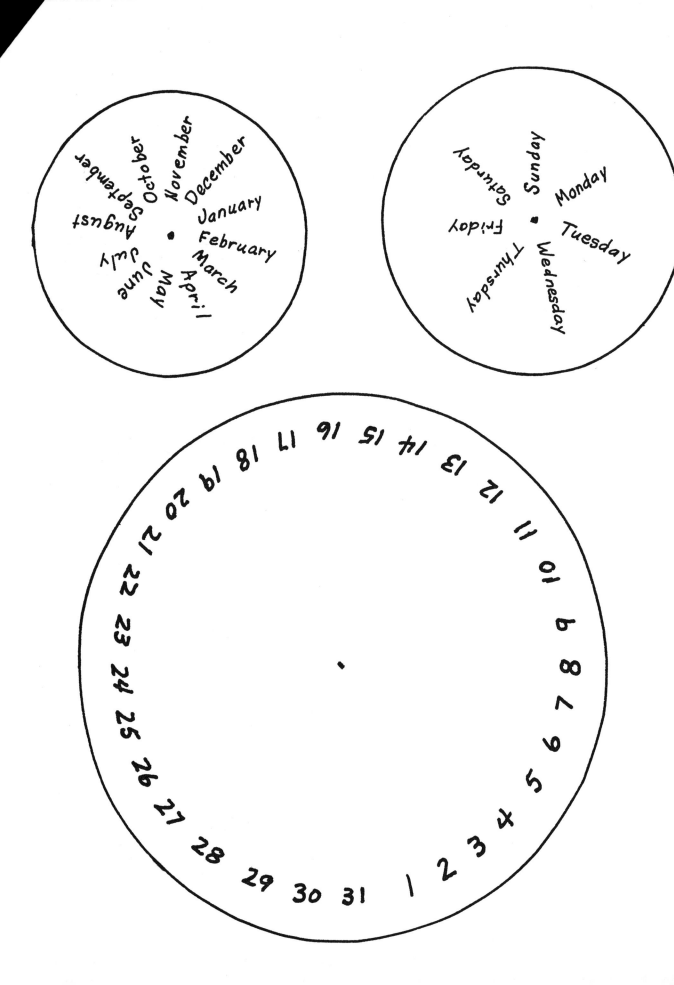

———— COLOR CHANGE ————

Objectives: • Learn how colors change
  • See and enjoy random designs

Supplies: Small containers such as paint pans, one for each color
  Water

Materials: Newsprint sheets 9″ × 12″
  Food coloring or tempera paints
  Old newspapers for drying

Directions:

1. Put a small amount of water into each container and add a different color to each container.

2. Fold newsprint sheets in pleats, triangles, and/or squares.

3. Dip the edges of the folded paper into the colors.

4. Unfold, if possible, and lay on the newspaper to dry. If it gets too wet, wait until it dries before separating the layers.

5. When dry, use the paper for book covers, greeting cards, background for pictures, or other projects.

——— COWBOY ———

Objectives: • Fine motor practice
• Figure-ground recognition
• Following directions
• Body parts and clothing names (vest, bandana, gauntlet gloves)

Supplies: Crayons
Scissors
Glue
Sharp knife to cut slits (optional for the teacher)

Materials: Ditto sheet of cowboy printed on tan poster paper

Directions:

1. Distribute a copy of the cowboy pattern to each child.

2. Talk about body parts (head, shoulders, wrists); then talk about clothing (hat, vest, bandana, gauntlet gloves).

3. Have children color both sides of the pattern using crayons.

4. Cut out the arm pieces, and color the back of them the same as the front.

5. Form the body by bringing the sides together, overlapping, and gluing at the dotted line.

6. Cut the slits for the arms.

7. Fold the arm pieces, but do not crease the fold. Insert them into the slits; then press out the tab ends to hold them in place.

8. Add facial features unless this was done when the pieces were colored.

Note: If you prefer, the arms may be glued on by folding the tabs toward the hands. Be sure the tabs are colored on the back side only, or the glue may not hold.

COWBOY

right

left

COWBOY PICTURE

Objectives:
- Eye-hand coordination
- Measuring and drawing with a ruler
- Sequencing by following directions
- Spatial organization
- Body parts

Supplies:
Pencils
Rulers
Scissors
Glue

Materials:
Manila poster or construction paper, 12″ × 18″, for background
Poster or construction paper, 4½″ × 6″ (quarter sheet of 9″ × 12″ paper);
one piece each in red, black, and blue or tan
Poster or construction paper 3″ × 4″, tan

Directions:

1. Measure 2″ from one of the short sides of the red piece; mark and cut off. Measure, mark, and cut this strip into two 1″ strips for the arms.

2. Trace all pattern pieces and cut them out.

3. Use leftover scraps of paper to cut out for eyes, mouth, belt, and hatband.

4. Glue the band on the hat, eyes and mouth on the face, and gloves on the arms.

5. Arrange all of the pieces on the background, and glue in place.

Note: The children might like to add to the background by using crayons to draw in hills, trees, or other things found on a ranch.

COWBOY PICTURE

cut 2

EASY BOOKMARK

Objectives: • Visual motor practice
• Measuring and angle recognition
• Fine motor control

Supplies: Scissors
Glue
Pencils
Sharp knife to cut slits (optional for the teacher)

Materials: Construction paper, any color 1/2″ × 24″
Small pieces of paper in two contrasting colors
Patterns for circles and flower shape

Directions:

1. Discuss measuring and right angles.

2. Distribute materials and supplies. Set aside small pieces of paper.

3. On the long piece of paper, measure 10½″ from one end and mark it lightly.

4. Using the mark for a guide, fold the strip at a 90° angle.

5. Fold the long remaining end of the strip so that it is parallel to the first side. This will make a point where the folds meet.

6. Trace and cut the larger circle from a small piece of paper. The teacher cuts a slit across the center of the circle, slightly longer than 1″.

7. Pull the pointed end of the folded strip through the slit.

8. Trace the flower shape on paper of another color and cut it out.

9. Trace three of the small circles and cut them out.

10. Glue one of the small circles in the center of the flower shape, onto the place where the strips and the slit in the circle come together.

11. Cut the ends of the strips to a point, and glue one of the small circles above each point.

Note: Other materials may be used to make the bookmarks, such as heavy cloth that does not ravel, Ultrasuede™, or felt. If leather pieces are available, they would make very attractive bookmarks. The trims could also be changed; instead of a flower, another shape could be used, and it could include a monogram.

EASY BOX

Objectives:
- Fine motor control
- Following directions
- Seeing cause and effect in construction

Supplies: Pencils
Scissors
Glue

Materials: Construction or poster paper, gift wrap, foil-backed paper, or wallpaper
Pattern

Directions:

1. Distribute supplies and materials.

2. Trace the pattern and cut out the box shape.

3. Fold and crease on all the dotted lines.

4. Glue side one over side two.

5. Fold in the short sides and tuck in the top flap.

6. Turn it over, fold in the short sides, and tuck in the bottom flap.

7. If desired, glue the bottom flap in place.

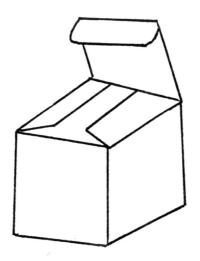

EASY BOX

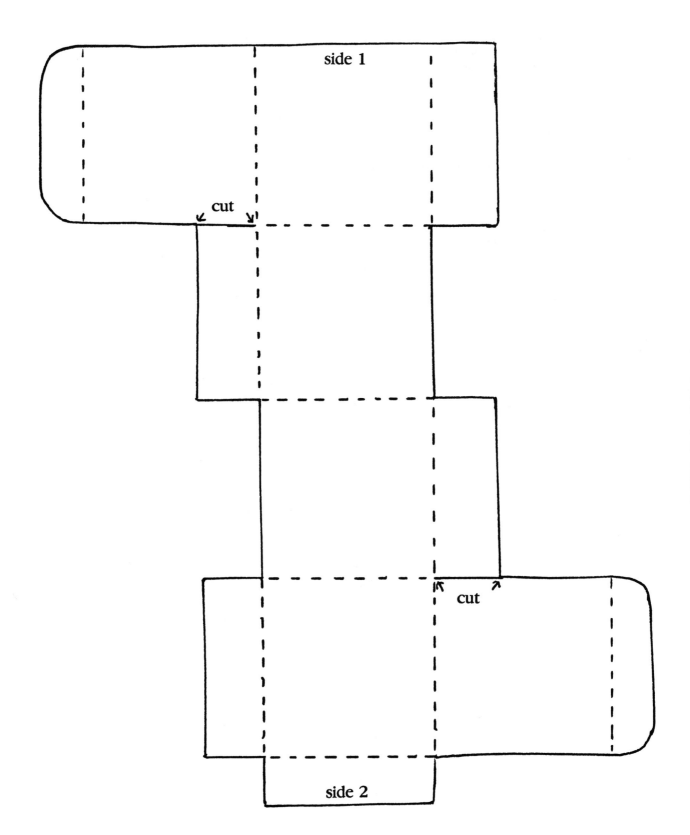

side 1

cut

cut

side 2

EVERYONE HAS A SHADOW

Objectives: • Visual perception
  • Perspective, effect of light source
  • Improve self-concept

Supplies: Pencils
  Scissors
  Glue

Materials: Construction paper 9″ × 12″ for background
  Poster or construction paper, light and dark colors
  Patterns

Directions:

1. Discuss what happens when we see our shadow. If the children are familiar with the story of Peter Pan, talk about how Peter felt when he lost his shadow. Discuss that everyone has a shadow. Another reference might be Robert Louis Stevenson's poem called "My Shadow" in *A Child's Garden of Verses*.

2. Distribute the supplies and materials. Trace and cut out the children and their shadows.

3. Arrange the pieces in the proper positions on the background, and glue in place.

SHADOWS

———— FLOWER POT ————

Objectives: • Understanding time limits
  • Exercising patience
  • Visual motor control

Supplies: Plaster of Paris
  Container for mixing and a spoon
  Paper or smooth plastic cups or plastic watercolor pans
  Tempera paint (optional)
  Dowels and petroleum jelly (optional)

Directions:

1. Before mixing the plaster, decide if you want to color it with the dry tempera paint. Then mix according to the directions on the container, and fill the cups.

2. If you have not made the flower, tree, or whatever will be used in the pot, you will need dowels that have been coated with petroleum jelly to insert in the pot.

3. The pots may be painted or covered with paper when they are dry.

   *The reason for using flexible plastic containers is so that the pot can be removed when it is dry.

Note: These pots can be used as a weighted base for many constructions that need to stand up independently.

——— FLOWER STRINGS ———

Objectives: • Fine motor coordination
  • Learning to fold and cut without patterns
  • Learning to use a needle and thread

Supplies: Scissors
  Needle
  Thread

Materials: Tissue paper, choice of colors, 2″ or 3″ squares

Directions:

1. Demonstrate folding the paper in quarters; then fold to form a triangle.

2. Demonstrate cutting the open ends in either a pointed or scalloped pattern that will look like a flower shape when unfolded.

3. Distribute the paper and scissors and have the children cut out a number of flowers in various shapes.

4. Leaving a long end on the thread, punch the needle through the flower about 1/4″ from one edge and then back through the opposite side.

5. Continue adding flowers on the thread. There should be at least five.

Note: Other types of paper may be used if they are soft enough to fold and cut easily. Tissue, however, allows light to enhance the flower effect.

——— FOLDED BOX ———

Objectives: • Practice in measuring
• Following directions
• Fine motor control

Supplies: Rulers
Scissors
Pencils

Materials: Gift wrap, poster paper, colored typing or duplicating paper, or lightweight wallpaper; 5½″ square for the top and 5¼″ square for the bottom, for a 2¼″ box.

Directions:

1. Follow the diagram, matching the numbers there with the direction numbers. Using the ruler, from corner to corner mark an X in the center of the square. This will be on the inside.

2. Using the ruler, measure on two opposing sides 1½″, and make a small mark.

3. Using the marks made in step 2, draw lines 1¾″ long and cut them.

4. Fold all four corners to the center.

5. Fold all sides to the center again, starting with 5a.

6. Unfold sides 6 and refold under sides 5a.

7. Press all four points into the center of this half of the box.

8. Using the other square of paper, repeat the directions to complete the top and bottom of the box.

9. If the paper is a little stiff or the folds are not too precise, it may be necessary to glue the points.

outside

inside

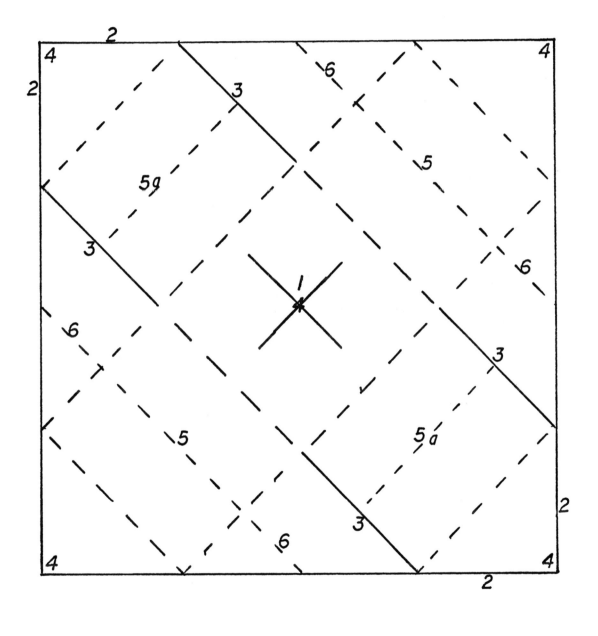

——— GEOMETRIC PATTERNS ———

Objectives: • Figure-ground recognition
                 • Using imagination
                 • Color coordination, effect of light and dark

Supplies: Pencils
                Scissors
                Rulers and protractors, if making patterns
                Glue

Materials: Poster or construction paper in dark and light colors
                Manila or other paper for background
                Patterns, if children are not making their own
                Lightweight cardboard or plastic for patterns

Directions:

1. Discuss color combinations and illustrate how patterns show up better when there is a contrast.

2. If the children are making their own patterns, distribute materials and give them a list of sizes and shapes: 2″ square, 1″ × 2″ rectangle, and triangle with 2³/₄″ base and 2″ sides.

3. Trace and cut pieces from light and dark colored paper: four triangles of each color, one to five squares, and four rectangles of each color.

4. Have the children try different arrangements of the shapes and colors.

5. When the desired design has been formed, glue the pieces onto the background paper. Start at the center, making sure the first piece is parallel with the edge of the background paper.

Note: Ideas for colors and patterns may be found in quilt pattern books in public libraries. The finished designs make a nice sampler "quilt" for the bulletin board. They can also be used as placemats to take home or to be given to a local nursing home.

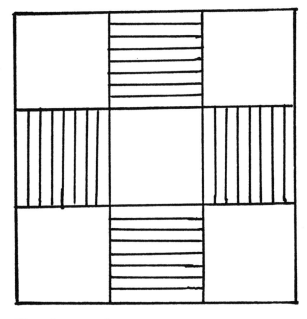

Simple, regular pattern

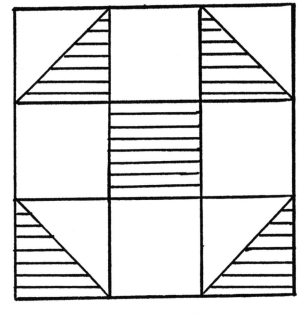

Simple pattern but irregular and lacks balance

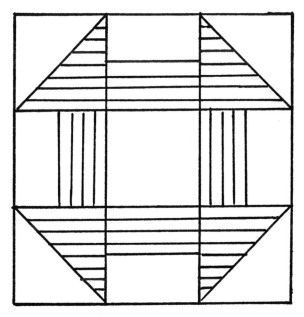

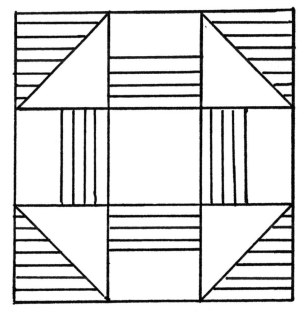

Two similar patterns show the effect of using light and dark colors for contrast

GIANT FLOWERS

Objectives: • Sequencing directions
• Fine motor control
• Cutting to shape without a pattern

Supplies: Scissors
Glue or other adhesive

Materials: Paper plates, 4″ or 6″ size
Construction paper, green, 1″ × 12″
Poster or construction paper, yellow or brown, 4″ square
Poster or construction paper, twelve pieces, 3″ × 6″, any flower color of your choice.

Directions:

1. Using the yellow or brown square of paper, round it off to form a circle.

2. Fringe the edges of the circle and glue to the bottom center of the paper plate for the center of the flower.

3. Shape the petals by rounding one end of the rectangle pieces and by cutting a long triangle from each side.

4. Turn the paper plate right-side-up and glue the petals to the sides, spacing them so there are no large gaps between the petals.

5. Glue the stem to the back of the flower.

Note: If you want the petals to be evenly spaced, glue two petals on opposite sides of the plate. Then turn the plate and glue two more opposite each other, dividing the plate into quarters. Fill each of the spaces with two petals. This might be a good time to work in some time-telling practice.

You might want to add leaves to the flowers. This can be done easily using 3″ × 6″ rectangles of green paper and cutting them in a leaf shape. A stiffer stem can be made by rolling a 2″ strip into a tube.

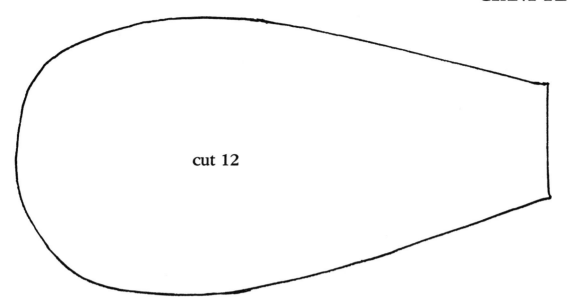

cut 12

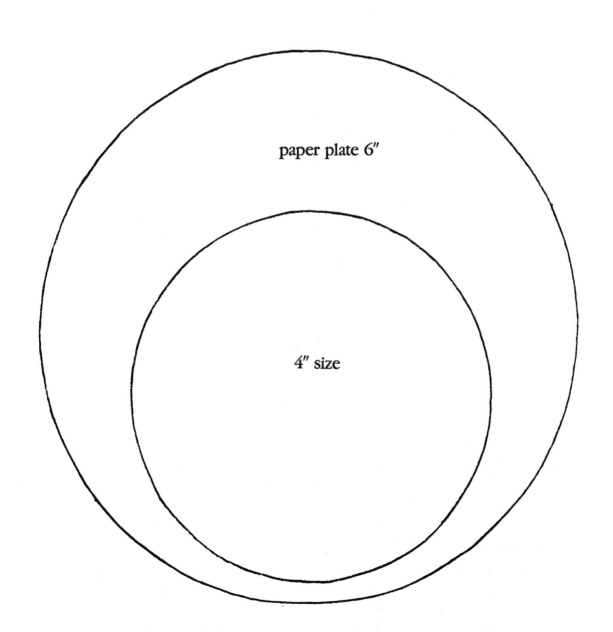

paper plate 6″

4″ size

———— GINGERBREAD DOLLS ————

Objectives: • Learn about traditions
            • Fine motor control
            • Visual perceptual coordination

Supplies: Pencils
           Scissors
           Glue (optional)
           Needle, heavy thread

Materials: Construction or poster paper or tagboard
           Cloth (optional)
           Patterns

Directions:

1. Discuss traditions for celebrating Christmas or other holidays. Gingerbread is a traditional cookie in many countries. References might also include stories in which gingerbread is included in some form.

2. Distribute supplies and materials. If using paper, trace and cut out several gingerbread boys and girls.

3. If using cloth, trace the pattern and cut out of tagboard. Rather than trying to trace on cloth, glue the cloth pieces to the tagboard and then trim off excess cloth after the glue dries.

4. Using the needle and thread, string the gingerbread children together, leaving a space between each of them. It is easier if the thread is passed across the back rather than cutting and tying each one.

5. Two sizes of patterns are included. The larger one might be used other than in a string. The gingerbread figures could even be converted to puppets.

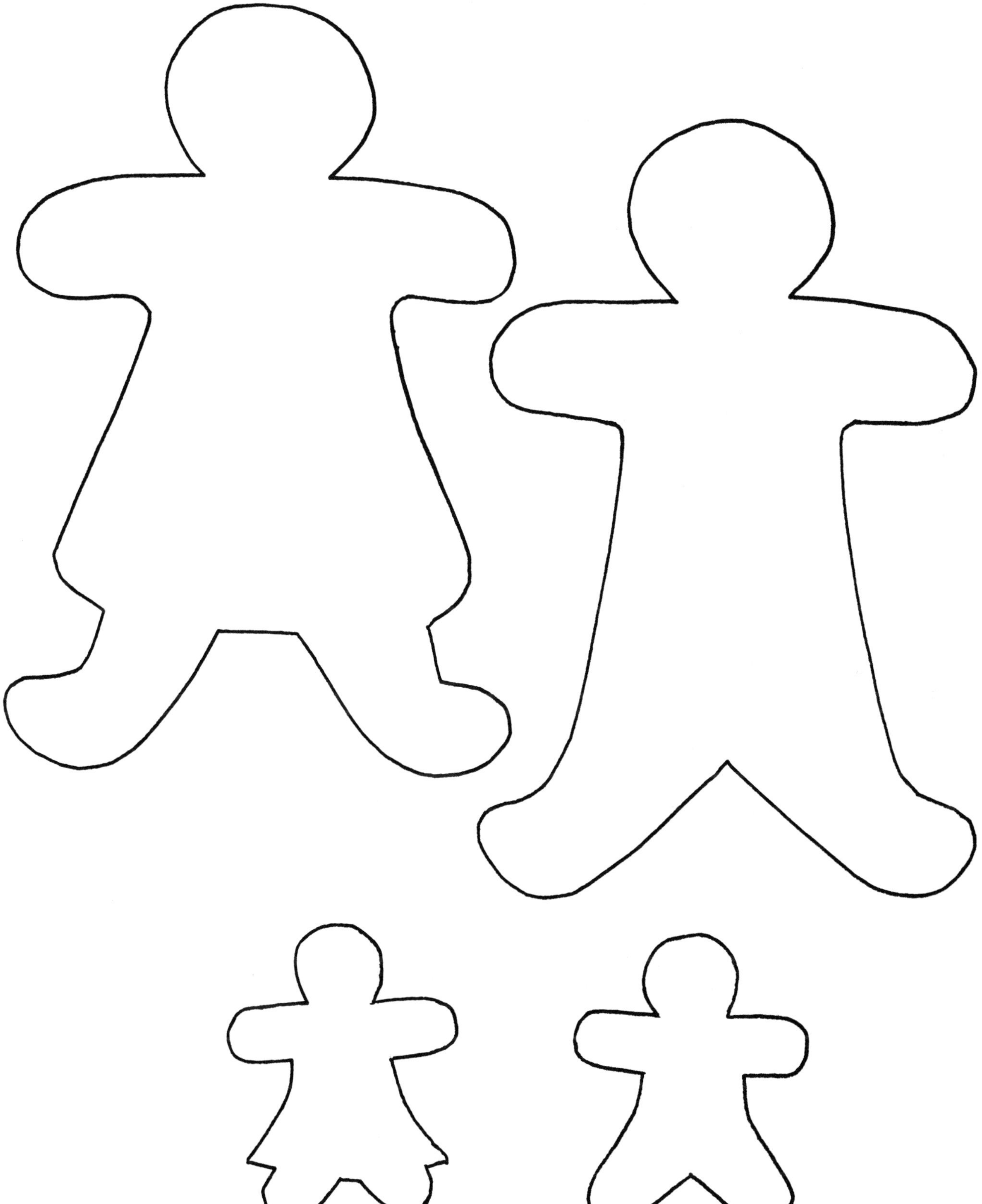

─── JUMPING JACKS ───

Objectives: • Eye-hand coordination
• Following directions
• Fine motor control

Supplies: Pencils
Scissors
Needle
Heavy thread
Crayons or colored pencils (optional)
Paper fasteners, 1/2" size

Materials: Construction paper, 9" × 12", white for the rabbit, tan or brown for the bear

Directions:

1. Discuss how jumping jacks move. Explain that they are toys usually made of wood.

2. Distribute supplies and materials for whichever jumping jack you are making.

3. Trace and cut out all the pieces.

4. Add features with pencils, crayons, or scraps of paper.

5. Fasten together loosely where the pattern is marked *f*. If it is difficult to fasten loosely enough for the parts to move easily, use a piece of cardboard to hold the pieces apart. Rotate the fastener to make a round hole.

6. For the rabbit, attach the heavy thread where the pattern is marked *s*, a single thread crossing from one ear to the other. Now attach a second thread in the center of the first. When you pull on this thread, the ears will move.

7. For the bear, attach a thread from front paw to front paw. Attach a second thread from rear paw to rear paw. Attach a third thread first to the thread on the front paws, and then to the thread connecting the rear paws. When the thread is pulled, all four paws will move.

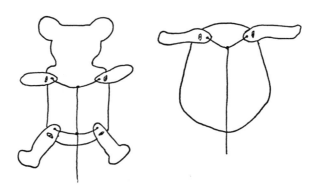

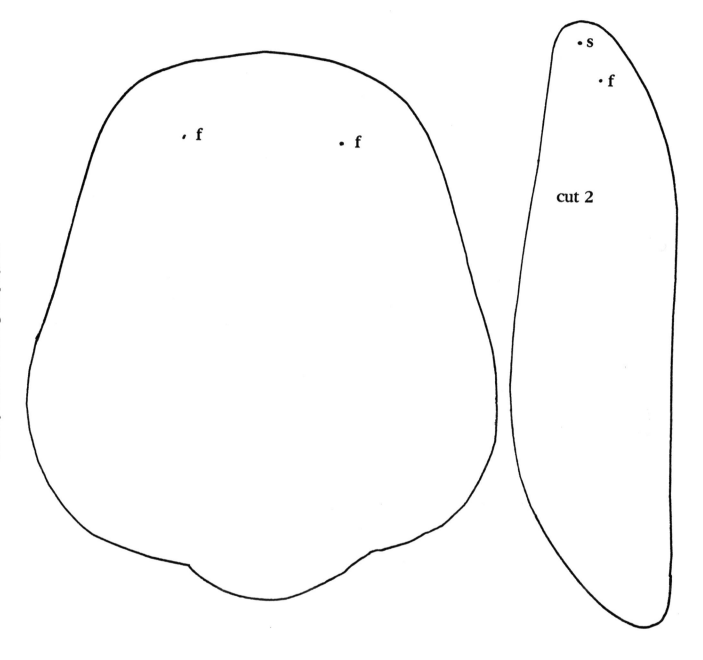

cut 2

JUMPING JACK

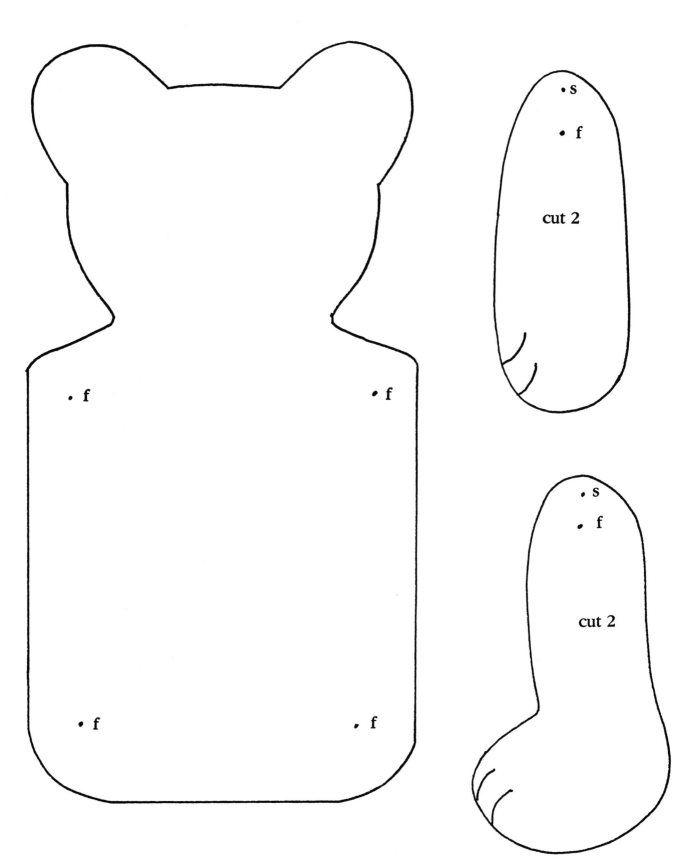

cut 2

cut 2

• s
• f

• s
• f

• f
• f

• f
• f

——— KALEIDOSCOPE ———

Objectives: • Vocabulary: kaleidoscope, symmetry, balance, dividing space
- Measurement, using protractor
- Listening and planning ahead
- Matching the sequence of a design

Supplies: Pencils
Scissors
Rulers
Glue
Protractors (72° sections)
Compass or 8½″ circle pattern

Materials: White tissue paper, at least 9″ square
Poster paper, five or six bright colors
Patterns for circles and triangles

Directions:

1. Talk about the vocabulary words and demonstrate using a kaleidoscope if one is available (or make a sample).

2. Distribute patterns and materials. Trace or draw the large circle with a compass and cut it out.

3. Using the protractor, divide the circle into five sections. Cut a small notch on the edge of each division and, using a pinhole in the center, draw lines to divide the circle.

4. Trace and cut out five each of a combination of shapes or half shapes. This will make five sets of matching pieces and colors.

5. Place the colored pieces on the circle as symmetrically as possible. Measure the spacing whenever possible.

6. Glue the pieces in place, adjusting any that may slip out of place in the process.

Note: Starting each section either in the center or at the outside edge will eliminate confusion. Use as little glue as possible to prevent tissue wrinkling.

If other material, such as acetate sheets, is available, it can be used for the circle. Be sure that your adhesive will bond to the material you use.

KALEIDOSCOPE

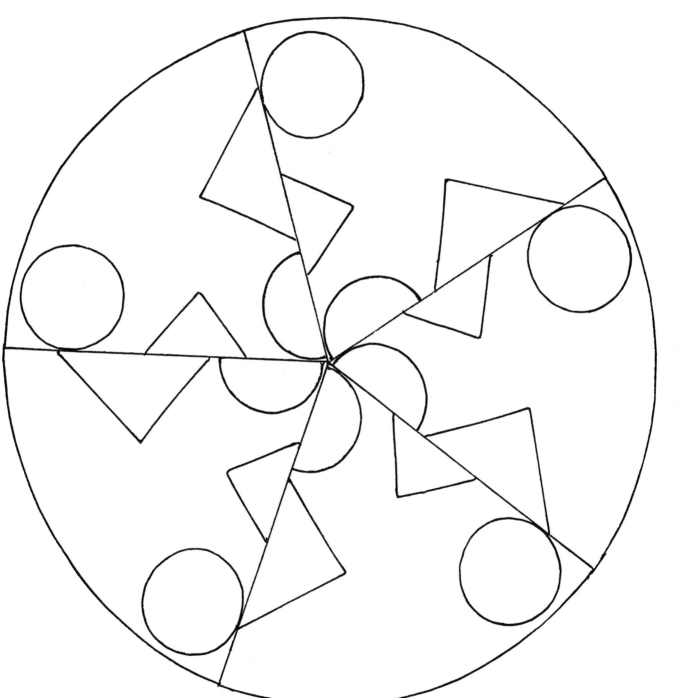

——— LAYERED PICTURE ———

Objectives: • Awareness of seasonal changes
   • Visual motor skills practice
   • Figure-ground discrimination
   • Sequence from parts to a whole

Supplies: Pencils
   Scissors
   Glue

Materials: Construction paper, 9″ × 12″, sky color according to the season represented
   Poster or construction paper, 3″, 4″, 5″, and 6″ by 12″ in shades of brown and/or green
   Brown poster paper 3″ × 9″ for tree trunks
   Poster paper in shades of green or other tree colors, according to season, amount determined by whether trees will all be the same color

Directions:

   1. Talk about seasons and which colors are appropriate for each time of year.

   2. Distribute materials and supplies.

   3. Using patterns placed on the edge of the paper, trace and cut out the layers of the picture.

   4. Glue the layers to the background, keeping them in the proper order.

   5. Using the appropriate paper, trace and cut out the clouds, tree trunks, and tree tops.

   6. Glue the clouds to the sky near the center. Do not worry if part of a cloud is covered by a tree top.

   7. Glue the trunks to the tree tops.

   8. The short tree is farther away, so place it in the midground part of the picture.

   9. Place the taller trees in the foreground.

   10. When the trees are in position, glue them in place.

Note: This picture originally had ten layers showing the rolling hills from the background to the foreground and was quite effective. If you would like to try something similar, move the first layer higher on the sky and fill in the spaces with layers of shaded papers, with one or two layers showing a little detail similar to the first two layers, but separated by curved hills. You could then place trees at several depths in the picture.

LAYERED PICTURE

layer 3

bottom of picture

layer 2, 4" to bottom

layer 4

bottom of picture

layer 1, 5" to bottom

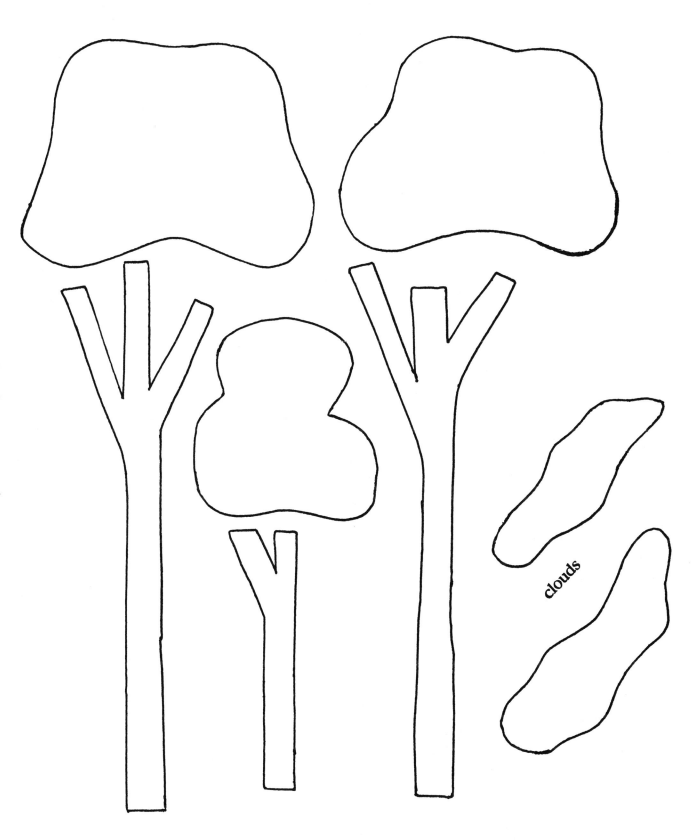

clouds

LEARNING TO CUT

Objectives: • How to hold scissors
• How to hold the paper
• How to turn the paper to cut a circle or to cut a straight line
• Recognition of shapes; how to make a square from a rectangle; how to make a triangle from a square

Supplies: Scissors

Materials: Several sheets or half sheets of newspaper or other paper of your choice for each child

Directions:

1. Demonstrate cutting, holding the scissors open wide and explaining that you want them to cut, not snip.

2. Have the children try holding the scissors to make random cuts.

3. Demonstrate holding the paper still to cut straight, and have the children do it.

4. Demonstrate turning the paper to cut curves and circles. Tell the children that fast turns make small circles. Let the children practice curves and circles.

5. Demonstrate cutting rectangles, squares, and triangles, and show how they can be changed into each other. Let the children practice these froms of cutting.

6. Let the children cut out some shapes and try putting them together to make people, animals, or whatever they imagine.

Note: After the children have had some fun cutting and trying some of their ideas, give them colored construction or poster paper and have them make pictures for the bulletin board or to take home.

MAGIC PICTURES

Objectives: • Visual perceptual control
• Cause and effect reinforcement
• Following directions

Supplies: Bottle of bluing
Large pan, not too deep
Rubber gloves

Materials: Duplicator or other firm paper
White crayons
Old newspapers and/or clothespins

Directions:

1. Talk with the children about what you will be doing, and emphasize that bluing can cause stains if not handled properly. Discuss how it will be possible to see a picture drawn with white on white.

2. Distribute paper and crayons. Suggest some ideas for pictures, such as things typical of Halloween or things typical of a winter scene.

3. Draw the pictures carefully using a moderate amount of pressure.

4. Meanwhile, using the rubber gloves, mix the bluing in just enough water to provide good coverage for dipping the pictures.

5. Carefully slide each picture into the water and wait a few seconds for the paper to color.

6. Carefully pull out the picture and let the water drip off; then place on newspaper to drain. When they are just damp, the pictures may be hung up with the clothespins to finish drying.

———— MAKING A BOOK ————

Objectives: • Following directions
• Eye-hand coordination
• Learning how things are made

Supplies: Dry mount press (optional)
Iron, if using dry mount (CAUTION: Iron to be used only under adult supervision)
Thinned white glue, and a glue brush
Scissors
Rulers
Pencils
Needle
Heavy thread

Materials: Paper or cloth and dry mount 12″ × 15″
Poster or construction paper, two pieces, 9″ × 12″
Light cardboard or chipboard, two pieces 6″ × 9″
Duplicator or typing paper, about five sheets

Directions:

1. If using dry mount, place it on the cloth or large sheet of paper, wrong-side-up, and use the iron to tack it in place.

2. Place the cardboard on the cover, evenly spaced, with about 1/2″ between the pieces. If using glue, mark where the cardboard will go, then brush the glue on, and put the cardboard back in place on the cover.

3. Fold the corners to the center and iron in place, or brush on glue to hold in place.

4. Fold the sides in and fasten in the same way.

5. Prepare the book pages by folding in half the two sheets of poster or construction paper and the five sheets of duplicator or typing paper.

6. On the inside of the fold, measure and mark the center at 4½″, and then measure 1¼″ twice on each side of the center; a total of five marks.

7. Using a large needle, punch holes at each mark.

8. Using the heavy thread, sew through the holes starting from the outside on one end. Sew back through the holes ending in the second hole from the outside. Tie the thread securely.

9. Glue the outside sheet of this page section to the cover of the book.

Note: The books may be personalized in several ways. Children can put their names on the cover, with or without a title. A bookplate can be made and glued to the inside cover. If the children have school pictures, a small one can be glued to the cover.

The books can be used in a number of different ways. They can be used as a diary or journal. To encourage reading, they can be used as a record of books the child has read. To encourage writing, the child can write stories or poems in the book. Some of the children might make the book into a picture book for a younger child or for themselves. Some schools develop a book-making- and writing program involving parents, who help print the books.

MONOFOLD FIGURES

Objectives: • Fine motor control
• Vocabulary: three-dimensional
• Sequencing parts to a whole
• Awareness of body parts, human and animal

Supplies: Scissors
Glue
Pencils (optional)

Materials: Paper—newsprint for practice; poster or construction paper in various sizes and colors
Cloth, yarn, or other bits and pieces depending on the project

Directions:

1. Talk about *three-dimensional*, and why it is necessary for things to be able to stand up.

2. Demonstrate by folding paper and cutting a shape that will stand alone. (See the sample in the following illustration.)

3. Practice drawing and/or cutting out shapes such as animals, or people from the waist down, with legs and feet large enough to stand.

4. Finish figures of people by adding a one-dimensional top, in one piece or in several fitted together.

5. Add features and details to animals and people.

Note: If the children show enthusiasm for this idea, it might be fun to construct a circus, a parade, a zoo, or self-images depicting the members of the class or the child's family.

MONOFOLD FIGURE

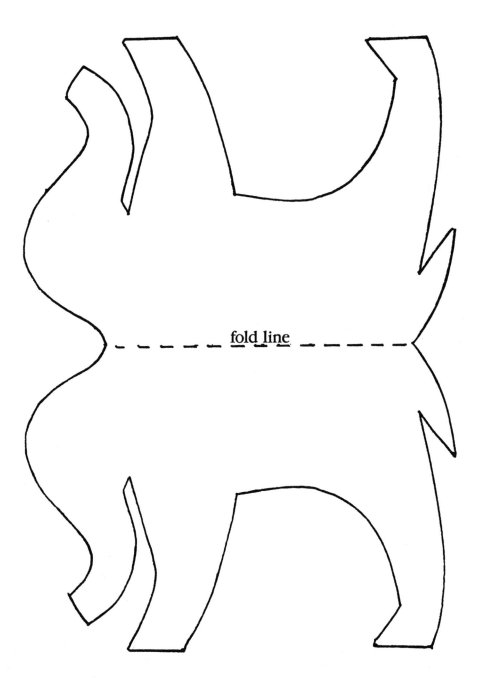

fold line

─── MOSAICS ───

A mosaic is a picture or design made from small pieces of colored paper. Examples can be seen in stained glass and floor tile.

Objectives: • Color vocabulary: blend, coordinate, contrast
               • Sequencing design and pattern
               • Directionality
               • Figure-ground association
               • Fine motor control

Supplies: Pencils
             Scissors
             Glue
             Rulers (optional)

Materials: Poster or construction paper for the background; size will depend on the project
Poster paper for the design; you choose colors
Newsprint or drawing paper

Directions:

1. Talk about the idea of a mosaic and give or show examples, such as pictures of floor tiles.

2. Talk about colors and demonstrate how they can be used to create a special effect. Use the vocabulary words.

3. Choose a subject or design and decide if it will be an individual or group project.

4. Using the newsprint or drawing paper, make sketches of the idea and decide what colors to use.

5. If rulers are to be used, begin to measure and cut the pieces. If the design is to be made from torn paper, talk about the size of the pieces and how to fit them together.

6. Arrange the pieces on the background to see if the design looks the way you thought it would.

7. When the design is satisfactory, glue the pieces in place.

Note: When you start to glue, it may be necessary to lay something on other pieces to keep them in place.

    An interesting mosaic can be made from paper tubes. Cut the tubes to lengths of 1¼″ to 1½″. Sketch a picture, perhaps a school mascot. Then, using a stiff background, transfer the picture into squares that have been drawn on the background. Next, cover the tubes with strips of paper in colors to complete the picture. The sketch can be colored with crayons to serve as a pattern for placing the pieces on the background. Making this three-dimensional mosaic exercises counting skills, builds cooperation, and improves self-image.

——— MURAL ———

Objectives:
- Working in a group
- Fine motor practice
- Recognition of shapes
- Organization and relationship of size to perspective
- Drawing and cutting without patterns
- Vocabulary: theme, mural

Supplies: Pencils
Scissors
Glue

Materials: Kraft paper for background (size and color will depend on the theme and where and how the mural will be displayed)
Poster paper in a variety of colors and sizes
Newsprint or other paper on which to sketch the ideas

Directions:

1. Explain the project and ask children to discuss a theme and how to carry it out in the mural.

2. Divide the class into groups of two to four.

3. Groups work on different parts of the mural. First make a sketch. Then make the pieces to go on the mural.

4. Begin assembling when the parts are ready. Discuss the best way to show depth by arranging bigger items closer to the center or bottom of the picture.

Note: It may work out better to let each group complete a part of the mural and then put the parts together rather than having the whole class working on one background at the same time. If the mural is showing seasons, it could be made in four panels. A park theme could show different areas of the park—playground, picnic area, ball diamond, nature trail, etc.

─── NEEDLEPOINT-TYPE CARDS ───

Objectives:
- Following directions
- Figure-ground recognition
- Color recognition
- Improving concentration
- Practice in counting

Supplies: Colored pencils or sharp crayons (erasable)
Scissors
Glue

Materials: ¼" ruled paper (graph, quadrille, or cross section)
Poster or construction paper, appropriate size for a card

Directions:

1. Beginning with the second square on the top, left side, number each square across the distance necessary for the pattern.

2. Beginning with the second row, left side, number each square down the first column as far as needed for the pattern.

3. Give the children copies to follow, or read the color and numbers to the class. Example: row 2, number 10, color green; row 3, numbers 9, 10, 11, color green.

4. When the coloring is finished, cut out the picture, leaving one row of blank squares all around the outside of the shape.

5. Distribute the paper for the card. Fold in half.

6. Glue the picture on the front of the card. Remind children that the fold is on the left side.

Note: This idea can be used for any occasion by choosing an appropriate picture. If you do not want to make cards, the same idea can be used for a picture, as part of a poster, or as a game when the children are not told what the picture will be when finished.

NEEDLEPOINT-TYPE CARDS

| | 1 | 2 | 3 | 4 | 5 | 6 | 7 | 8 | 9 | 10 | 11 | 12 | 13 | 14 | 15 | 16 | 17 | 18 | 19 |

X green
X brown
X other colors

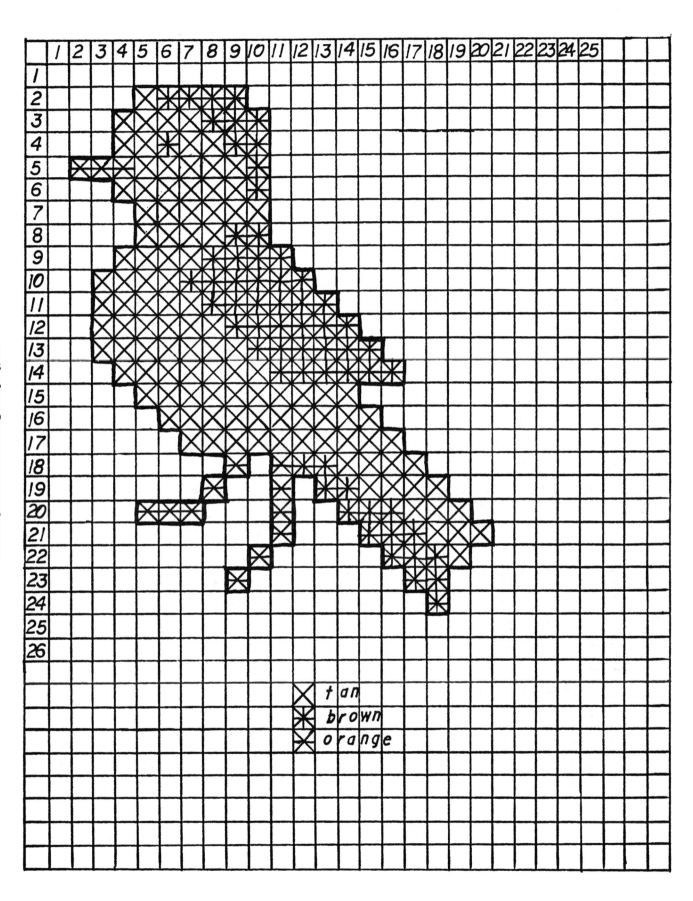

NEEDLEPOINT-TYPE CARDS

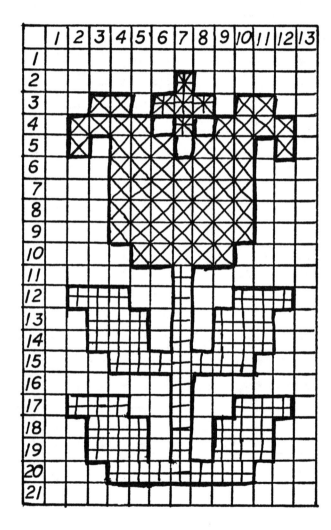

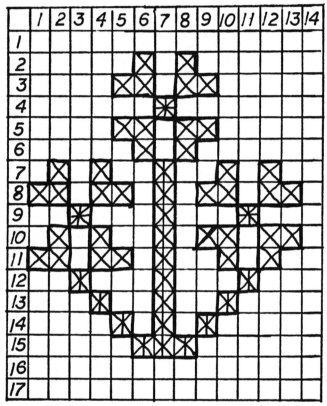

———— OWL ————

Objectives: • Fine motor coordination
            • Following directions
            • Awareness of proportions

Supplies: Scissors
            Pencils
            Glue and paste
            Paper punch (optional)

Materials: Construction paper, orange or tan, 3″ × 5″
            Wallpaper, foil, or other contrasting paper, 3″ × 4″
            Small pieces of yellow and black poster paper
            Patterns for body, wings, and top of head

Directions:

1. Discuss why owl's eyes are usually thought to be very large—for example owls are nocturnal, and many varieties have feathers radiating around their eyes.

2. Distribute supplies, materials, and patterns.

3. On the orange or tan paper, trace and cut out the body.

4. On the contrasting paper, trace and cut out the rest of the pieces.

5. Glue the top of the head and the wings in place.

6. Cut circles or ovals from the yellow paper; set aside.

7. Use a large paper punch or cut by hand small circles from the black paper, and glue them on the yellow circles.

8. Cut a triangle from the black paper for a beak.

9. Glue the eyes and beak in place.

OWL

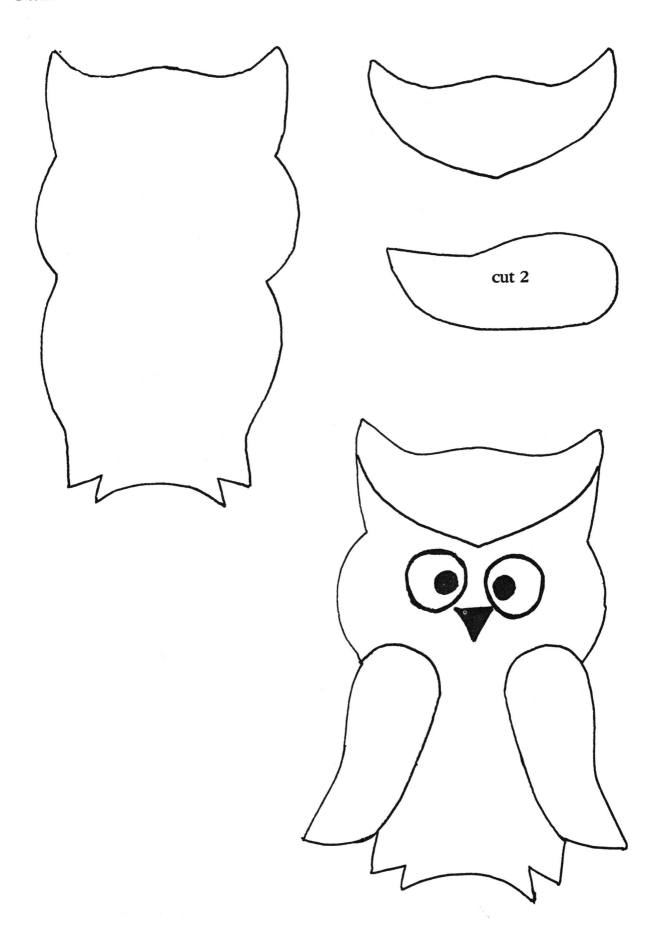

cut 2

————— PAPER BAG COVERS —————

Objectives: • Showing cause and effect
• Following directions
• Following safety rules

Supplies: Rulers
Pencils
Crayons
Scissors
Iron (CAUTION: Iron to be used only under adult supervision)
Glue

Materials: Brown paper bags or kraft paper
Poster paper or gift wrap for mounting
Plain newsprint

Directions:

1. Discuss how we can make something look like something else. In this case, we will make brown paper look like leather.

2. Distribute the paper bags and cut them open. Trim off the edge where the bag was glued, and discard the bottom.

3. Using crayons, if desired, color the paper or parts of the paper. Do not color too heavily or you will not get the dyed color effect of leather.

4. Crumple the paper. Spread out and crumple many times until it is a mass of small lines and feels soft.

5. Place the paper between sheets of newsprint to absorb the excess crayon. Then press with a medium-hot iron to smooth it out enough to use.

6. Measure and cut the paper to the desired size for a book cover, note paper, or other use.

7. Glue it carefully to the background.

——— PAPER TIE DYE ———

Objectives: • Seeing cause and effect
• Hand-eye coordination
• Using preventive caution

Supplies: Small containers for paint
Tempera paints, two or three colors
Colored pencils or fine-tip felt pens, black or harmonizing with paint color

Materials: White paper towels
Old newspapers
Construction paper or tagboard for mounting

Directions:

1. Mix or pour out small amounts of paint in small containers. Remind the children that paint can stain their clothes.

2. Distribute the paper towels and have each child fold them in whatever manner they choose.

3. Taking turns, let the children dip the corners of the folded towel into one or two colors of paint.

4. Unfold the paper carefully and lay it on newspapers to dry. Wash hands if needed.

5. When the paper has dried, use a small amount of glue around the edges to mount it on a background. Be sure it is smooth so you will be able to write on it.

6. Use the colored pencils or felt-tip pens to copy a short verse either from something that children have written or from some other source.

Note: Haiku verse works well here. If the children have never tried this type of writing, they will enjoy the challenge of using three lines and seventeen syllables to express a thought or an observation of nature. There are some excellent books of Haiku that can be used either for inspiration or for a verse to copy.

One group of children used two squares of the dyed paper as covers for a long strip of paper folded into four sections, with a Haiku for each season:

Sunshine and shadows
Clouds floating across spring skies
Happy time of year.

Flowers bloom, birds sing
Long days, happy and busy
Summer time, fun time.

Skies gray, leaves dropping
Harvest, pumpkins, and corn shocks
Color fading, fall.

Icy winds, snow falls
Frosty morning Bright noontime
Winter nips at us.

———— PEOPLE SPRINGS ————

Objectives: • Visual motor coordination
• Eye-hand control
• Using imagination

Supplies: Pencils
Scissors
Glue
Crayons, colored pencils, or fine-tip felt pens

Materials: Poster paper, 1/2" wide, some strips 18" to 24" long, others random lengths
Small pieces of construction or poster paper, colors and sizes according to use
Patterns for heads, if needed

Directions:

1. Before starting the project, be sure all the children know how to fold paper to achieve the accordion effect, which is the spring for the body of the people.

2. Distribute the supplies and materials.

3. Using two long strips of paper, fold to make the spring, glue the ends and trim off any excess.

4. Glue a strip of paper 4½" to 5" long across one end for the arms, and another strip about 6" long across the other end for legs.

5. Cut a short tab on one end of an oval or round piece of paper. Crease and glue the tab to the top of the spring. This is the head.

6. The character chosen determines what features are needed to complete the head. Examples: A head for a Santa Claus could have the hat as part of a background piece with a face added on one side. This gives the appearance of a cap on the back of the head. In the same way, a background piece could be used to represent hair. Other features might be shoes or feet, heads or mittens.

Note: These little characters can be used in a number of ways: as ornaments for the Christmas tree, players for a puppet play, a rabbit for spring (just add ears), as part of an information poster, or whatever can be imagined.

PEOPLE SPRINGS

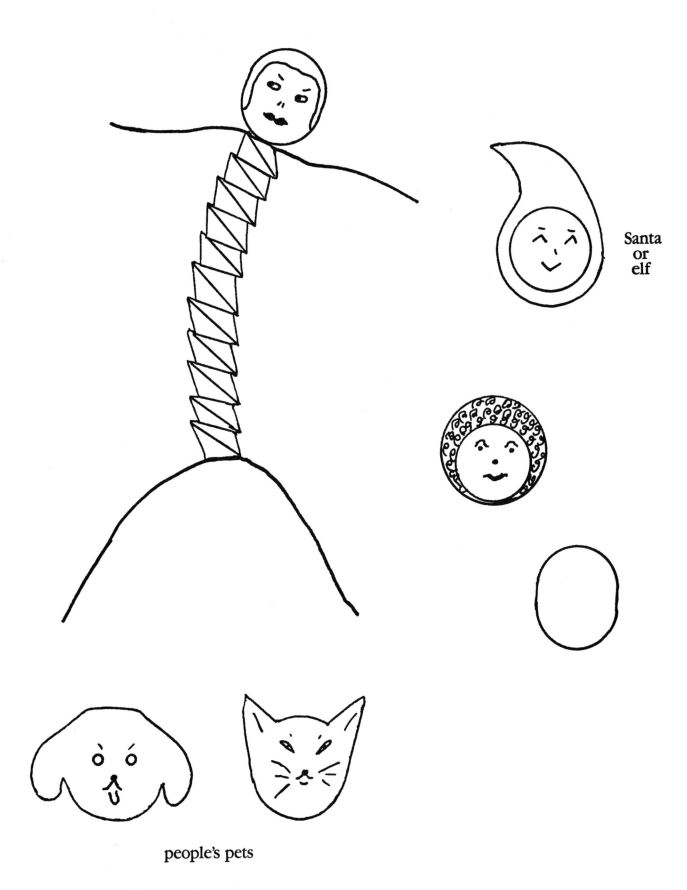

Santa
or
elf

people's pets

POEMS AND STORIES IN PICTURES

Objectives: • Multisensory perception
                • Visual and fine motor coordination
                • Using information imaginatively

Supplies: Pencils
              Scissors
              Glue

Materials: Construction and/or poster paper
               Other materials according to project

Directions:

1. There are many poems and stories that develop visual images. Some that are especially adaptable describe seasonal changes. Several could be read ahead of time to see which ones might interest the children in a creative way.

2. Panels can be made showing the seasonal changes in an apple tree: blooming in the spring; in the summer leaves with birds' nests in the branches; in the autumn ripe apples and leaves falling; in the winter bare branches.

3. Stories and/or poems can be depicted in panels, pictures, or murals. Sometimes a story or poem can be illustrated with geometric shapes similar to a mosaic.

4. Some poems and stories evoke color perceptions that can be carried out either in picture form or by using shades of the colors in random shapes.

QUILLING

Quilling is an old art form in which narrow strips of paper are rolled around a small cylinder, such as a dowel stick. It is taken off the tool and shaped with the fingers to produce a desired piece for a picture. In some cases the shaped paper resembles a quill or feather—thus the name of the process.

Quilling is adaptable to many projects—for example, pictures of birds, flowers, trees, or fantasy pictures. Quilling can also be used to make a frame for a small picture or a wreath for Christmas. The following are basic directions.

Objectives: • Fine motor control
• Eye-hand coordination
• Following directions

Supplies: Small dowels cut to about 3″ lengths, or round toothpicks (craft stores sell a quilling tool)
Glue or clear tape
Paper cutter

Materials: Poster paper, duplicator paper, or stationery, cut in 1/4″ strips
For practice, you might want to use 1/2″ strips and round pencils. This will not give a true quilling look, but can make some interesting projects.

Directions:

1. The basic method is to wrap the paper strips around the stick firmly until the full length of paper is used. At this time, relax your grip slightly to loosen the paper just enough to slide off the stick.

2. If you need a tight round shape, glue the paper before removing it from the stick.

3. If you are making a leaf shape, pinch the loose roll on one side to form a point.

4. Pinch both sides of a loosened roll to form two points for a leaf, petal, or feather.

5. Curl the pinched side to form a paisley shape.

6. The number, shape, and color of the pieces needed are best determined by following a sketch and laying the pieces on it.

loose roll

 "S" roll

tight roll

 scroll

 teardrop

 "V" roll

feather

 flat scroll

 eye

open heart

 curved leaf

 square

 heart

 tendril

QUILLING CARDS

Objectives: • Fine motor control
• Visual motor reinforcement

Supplies: Small dowels or round toothpicks
Scissors
Glue

Materials: Poster or other soft paper 1/4″ wide, about 9″ long
Paper doilies, 5″ size
Poster paper for background, about 3″ across
Patterns, if needed
Quilling samples

Directions:

1. Using a color such as yellow or light green, roll a tight piece for the flower center. Set this aside.

2. Using the main flower color, make five leaf-shaped petals. Set these aside.

3. Make two green, leaf-shaped rolls. Set these aside.

4. Glue the background paper to the doily.

5. Arrange the quilled pieces in a flower shape and glue in place on the background.

Note: The background color and shape will depend on the purpose of the card. For a valentine, the background should probably be a heart shape. For a Mother's Day card or a card for another holiday, the background could be a circle, heart, scalloped circle, or diamond shape. Quilling looks best if it is kept fairly dainty, since commercial quilling paper is usually about 1/8″ wide.

RECIPES: CLAY-TYPE MATERIALS

Children like to work with modeling materials. Clay-substitute materials need no special handling and do not need to be fired in a kiln. Color can be added to the mixtures, or they can be painted after drying at room temperature or in a kitchen oven. These materials can be handled in much the same way as real clay.

Objectives: • Fine motor skills
   • Visual motor development
   • Stimulate creative abilities

CREPE CLAY

Supplies: Large bowl
Scissors
Measuring cup
Spoon

Materials: One fold of crepe paper, any color
1 tablespoon table salt
1 cup flour
Water

Directions:

1. Cut the crepe paper in confetti-size paper. Place in the bowl and add just enough water to cover the paper.

2. Soak for fifteen minutes; then pour off the excess water.

3. Mix flour and salt and add enough to crepe paper to make a stiff dough.

4. Knead well until blended with the crepe paper.

Note: You might want to wear light-weight rubber gloves for the kneading process since crepe paper color bleeds when wet.

FLOUR CLAY 1

Supplies: Measuring cup
Large bowl
Fork or spoon for mixing

Materials: 4 cups self-rising flour
1 cup table salt
1½ cups water

Directions:

1. Mix flour and salt in the bowl. Slowly add water; mix to form a ball.

2. Knead the dough for five to ten minutes. Add water if it is too dry, and add flour if dough is sticky.

3. You may store the dough in plastic in the refrigerator for up to five days.

4. You may dry the clay for several days at room temperature or bake it in a 300° oven for one to two hours.

FLOUR CLAY II

Supplies: Measuring cup and spoon
Large bowl
Fork or spoon for mixing

Materials: 1 cup flour
1 cup table salt
1 rounded teaspoon alum powder (available in a grocery store or pharmacy— it is used for some types of pickling)
Water

Directions:

1. Mix the dry ingredients and add water slowly.

2. Knead until you reach a clay-like consistency.

SAWDUST MODELING MATERIAL 1

Supplies: Large bowl
Fork or spoon for mixing

Materials: Fine sawdust
Wallpaper paste (wheat paste)
Water

Directions:

1. Mix equal parts of the ingredients.

2. If it is sticky, add more sawdust.

SAWDUST MODELING MATERIAL II

Supplies: Large bowl
Fork or spoon for mixing
Measuring cup

Materials: 2 cups sawdust
1 cup plaster of Paris
1/2 cup wheat paste or wallpaper paste
2 cups water

Directions:

1. Mix dry ingredients and add water slowly until you reach modeling consistency.

2. Use this for puppet heads, artificial fruits and vegetables, masks, and animal or people figures.

──── SAFETY SHAPES ────

Objectives: • Reinforce safety practices
• Using shapes for identification
• Visual motor integration

Supplies: Pencils
Scissors
Rulers
Crayons, colored pencils, or felt-tip pens
Glue (optional)

Materials: Construction or poster paper 9″ × 12″, colors appropriate for the signs
Pattern shapes

Directions:

1. Discuss the various kinds of signs that provide clues for safety: stop sign or traffic signals; caution signs—no bicycles, slow, yield, railroad crossing; information signs—crossings, street names; other signs appropriate for the area where the children live.

2. Show the patterns without lettering or pictures. If the children are making their own patterns, this will show them what shapes they will need.

3. Distribute supplies and materials. Trace or draw and cut out the shapes from appropriate colored paper.

4. Add the details so the signs can be read.

5. The signs may be left as is, or they may be arranged as a poster.

6. If the signs are being made for a special safety campaign, the children might like to write slogans to go with the signs.

———— SHAPE FACES ————

Objectives: • Shape recognition and identification
• Fine and visual motor coordination
• Using imagination

Supplies: Pencils
Scissors
Glue
Fine-tip markers (optional)
Paper punch (optional)

Materials: Poster or construction paper in a variety of colors, 3″ × 4″ and 4″ × 5″
Poster paper scraps in a variety of colors
Shape patterns

Directions:

1. Talk about and show shapes; name and define them.

2. Talk about different shapes of faces—animals, real people, and fantasy people or animals.

3. Distribute patterns and paper. Trace the shapes, one of each to start.

4. Using the scrap paper, cut (freehand) features for each face and glue in place. Fine-tip markers may be used to emphasize features such as eyelashes.

Note: The finished people faces may be used to make a picture of the child's family, and the animal faces can be mounted as a picture in the zoo or on the farm. Add some line drawings in or around the faces to finish the picture.

—— SHAPE PICTURES OR SILHOUETTES ——

Objectives: • Vocabulary suggestions: shapes, silhouette, color coordination and arrangement
              • Figure-ground recognition
              • Fine motor reinforcement
              • Visual motor integration

Supplies: Scissors
Glue

Materials: Black or white construction paper, 9″ × 12″ or 6″ × 9″, for background
Shapes copied on white or colored paper

Directions:

1. Talk about the suggested vocabulary words to establish shape recognition, the meaning of *silhouette*, how colors affect each other, and the results of arrangement of shapes.

2. Cut out all of the shapes. If you are using only two colors, black and white, for a true silhouette the small background will usually work best.

3. If you are using more colors, up to four will work well on a larger background.

4. Arrange the shapes on the background and move them around until you like the picture.

5. Glue the shapes in place.

Note: This picture can be shown to good advantage by giving it a simple frame. Shallow boxes, such as those pantyhose sometimes come in, can be used; or strips of construction paper can be folded to form miter corners for a frame. More elaborate frames can be constructed from wallpaper—metallic, woven or bamboo replicas, or small prints look best.

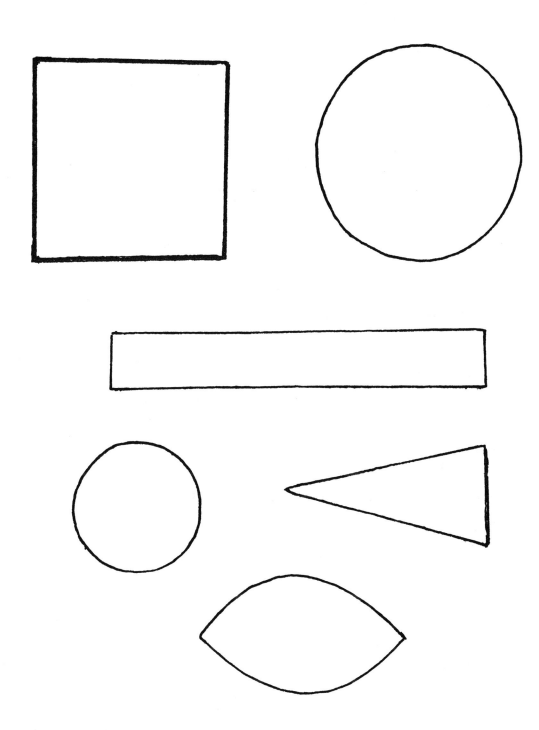

———— SHIPSHAPE ————

Objectives: • Recognition of square and triangle
• Visual motor integration
• Fine motor control

Supplies: Pencils
Scissors
Glue
Rulers, if making patterns
Crayon or felt-tip pen

Materials: Construction paper, 9″ × 12″ for background, sky color
Construction or poster paper, 2″ × 12″, blue-green for water
Poster or construction paper, 4½″ × 4″, white
Poster or construction paper, 4½″ × 4″, color of choice
Patterns for squares and triangles

Directions:

1. Distribute supplies and materials.

2. If using rulers, measure to make 2″ squares, using both white paper and paper for the boat. Then divide some of both into triangles.

3. If using patterns, trace and cut out four triangles from the white paper for sails and two squares and two triangles for the boat. Set them aside.

4. Prepare the background by tearing one side of the length of the blue-green paper. Glue it to the background sky color.

5. Arrange the boat pieces over the water and glue in place.

6. Using the felt-tip pen, draw two lines for masts, about 5″ long.

7. Arrange the sails on the masts and glue in place.

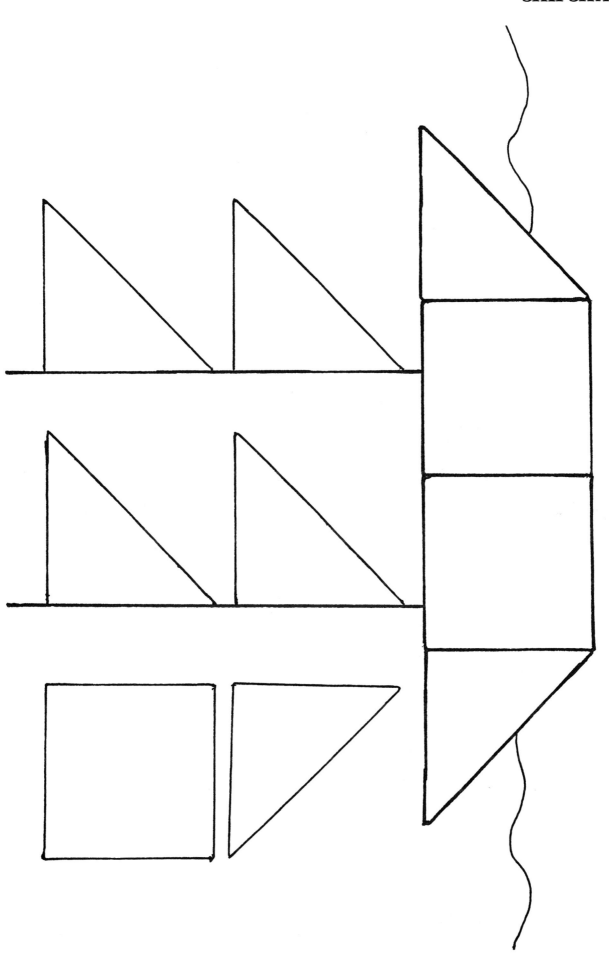

——— SIMPLE PUPPET ———

Objectives: • Learning cause and effect
            • Practice visual motor skills
            • Increase observation skills
            • Practice measuring

Supplies: Pencils
            Scissors
            Glue or paste
            Rulers

Materials: Poster paper, flesh color, 4″ × 12″
            Small pieces of paper for details
            Yarn in hair colors, if desired

Directions:

1. Talk with the children about actions that cause other things to happen. Example: If we draw a mouth on our finger and thumb, movement makes it look as if the mouth is speaking.

2. Distribute the supplies and materials.

3. Using scissors, round off the corners on one end of the strip of paper.

4. Using the ruler, measure from the rounded end and mark at 3″, 4½″, and 6″.

5. Fold the paper across at the 4½″ mark.

6. Fold back at the 3″ and 6″ marks so there is a 1½″ double fold on one side of the strip of paper.

7. Draw and cut out lips (upper and lower) and glue to the edge of the 3″ and 6″ folds on the opposite side from the double fold.

8. Cut hair from scrap material or use yarn. Glue in place.

9. Draw and cut out eyes and glue in place.

10. Cut two strips of paper 1″ × 3″. Glue these on the back of the puppet on the double fold. Glue them so that they allow space for the fingers to operate the mouth.

11. When the glue is dry, operate the puppet by placing the thumb in the space of the lower strip on the double fold and the first finger in the upper space.

Note: The puppets may be changed by adding other details. For example, they may be made to represent characters in a story or to look like animals. Pictures of animals may be glued onto the basic puppet shape. This is a good project to enhance self-concept.

fold forward ___ ___ ___ ___ 1   Folds 1 and 2 come together in front

fold backward ___ ___ ___ ___   Strips for fingers on back of this fold

fold forward ___ ___ ___ 2

measure to 12″

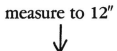

——— SPOON FINGER PUPPET ———

Objectives: • Fine motor control
              • Sequencing and following directions
              • Building self-concept

Supplies: Pencils
            Scissors
            Glue
            Colored pencils or fine-tip felt pens
            Flat wooden ice cream spoons

Materials: Poster paper 3″ × 5″ for clothing
             Poster paper or yarn in hair colors
             Cardboard, such as tablet back, if spoons are not available
             Patterns

Directions:

1. If spoons are not available, use the pattern; trace and cut out the spoon shape.

2. Using colored pencils or felt-tip pens, draw the features for the face on the large end of the spoon.

3. Trace and cut out the other pieces. On the boy's clothes, do not cut out the triangle unless you glue a piece of black paper behind it so the finger will not show.

4. Fold the clothing piece around the neck and glue the full length, but do not glue it to the spoon.

5. Position the arms on the back and glue in place.

6. Glue the hair around the face. Then glue on the back hair.

Note: You can make many changes on each puppet to individualize them. Hair shape can be changed, or yarn can be used for hair. The clothes can be trimmed in many ways. Legs and/or feet may be added as well as hands. Also, depending on the size of the child, the length of the clothes can be varied to fit the finger size. The puppets can represent storybook characters or family members, depending on how they will be used.

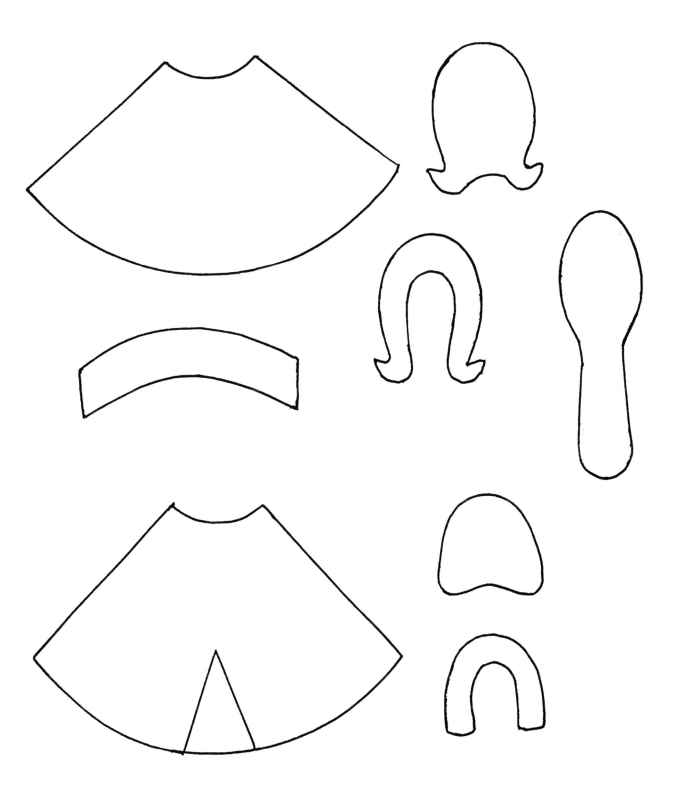

————— STAINED-GLASS DESIGNS —————

Objectives: • Listening and following directions
  • Using colors for a special effect
  • Practicing patience rather than gaining immediate gratification

Supplies: Paintbrushes
  Paint pans or small jars
  Liquid starch
  Pencils
  Scissors
  Paper punch
  Thread for hanging

Materials: Tissue paper, 2″ squares
  Waxed paper
  Patterns

Directions:

1. Tear off a square of waxed paper, at least 8″ square.

2. Select two or three colors of tissue paper.

3. Using little dots of starch, stick the tissue paper to the waxed paper.

4. When the waxed paper is covered with the tissue squares, paint over the whole surface with a thin coating of the liquid starch.

5. Repeat steps 3 and 4 until three layers of tissue cover the waxed paper.

6. Dry at least overnight.

7. Cut out designs or use patterns of your choice to trace and cut out designs.

8. Punch a hole near one edge and insert thread for a hanger.

Note: A number of different things can be made from the stained-glass piece, such as Christmas ornaments, turkeys for Thanksgiving, or spring flowers. Be careful to choose a shape that does not have small cuts on the edges, since this paper is very brittle.

A sun catcher using any geometric shape can be made by cutting a frame from construction paper, a little larger than the stained glass. Then cut out the center so it will overlap the stained glass. The sun catcher looks best if the stained glass is sandwiched between two frames.

STICK AND CIRCLE FLOWERS

Objectives: • Reinforce shape recognition
 • Sequence directions
 • Fine motor coordination

Supplies: Pencils
 Scissors
 Glue
 Stir sticks (the narrow, wooden kind)

Materials: Patterns (or compass for older children) for 1¼" circle and 2" circle
 Poster or construction paper in leaf and flower colors

Directions:

1. Trace and cut out one 2" circle in white or your choice of color for the background of the flower.

2. Trace and cut out six small circles for the flower petals.

3. Trace and cut out one small circle for the center of the flower.

4. Trace and cut out two small circles from green paper.

5. Glue the center to the background. Space the six petals around the center and glue in place.

6. Glue the flower to one end of a stir stick.

7. Glue the green circle leaves in place lower on the stick.

Note: These flowers may be used on a bulletin board or taped on windows; or display them in small clay pots or juice cans that have been covered with paper or painted. Wadding newspaper or tissue under and around the stems will hold them erect. Brown tissue paper is best with the clay pots.

STICK AND CIRCLE FLOWERS

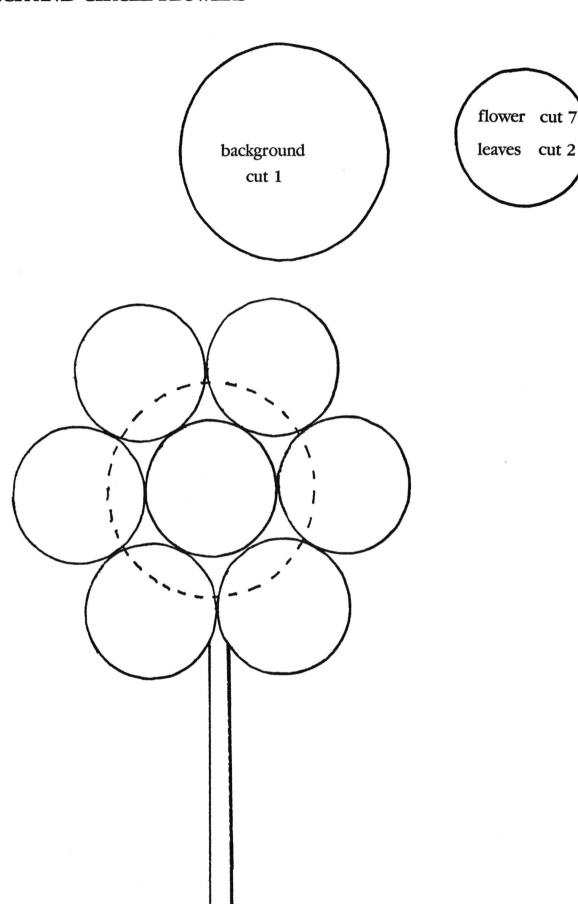

background
cut 1

flower   cut 7

leaves   cut 2

─── SUN CATCHERS ───

Objectives: • Following directions
• Color recognition and blending
• Visual and fine motor control

Supplies: Pencils
Scissors
Needle
Heavy thread or light string

Materials: Plastic, such as milk jugs or any plastic of similar weight
Felt-tip pens, black and bright colors
Patterns
Newspapers to work on

Directions:

1. If you are using plastic milk jugs, they will have to be cut apart ahead of time.

2. Distribute materials and papers.

3. Trace a pattern on the plastic and cut it out.

4. Lay the plastic cut-out on the newspaper and, using the black pen, trace around the edge.

5. Still using the black pen, mark off areas of the sun catcher so that other colors will be separated.

6. Using bright colors, carefully fill in the spaces.

7. When the first side is dry, turn it over and repeat the directions on the other side.

8. Using the needle, punch a hole and pull thread through for a hanger.

SUN CATCHERS

THREE-COLOR BOOKMARK

Objectives: • Color harmony
• Visual motor coordination
• Listening and following directions

Supplies: Scissors
Glue

Materials: Poster paper in a choice of colors, two strips $1\frac{1}{2}'' \times 8''$
Poster paper in harmonizing colors, one strip $2'' \times 8\frac{1}{2}''$

Directions:

1. Place the two smaller pieces of paper on top of each other, keeping the edges even.

2. Carefully fold the papers lengthwise. If it is easier, fold each piece of paper separately, being careful to fold them evenly so they will fit together smoothly.

3. Cut a design through the four thicknesses of paper from the fold side. The paper must be held firmly and the cuts be made carefully to prevent the cuts from being too close together or too near the edge.

4. Still keeping the two pieces together, unfold the paper and bend the designs to one side. This will leave a hole and the two colors of the tabs will be seen.

5. Glue the tabs of the design to the space on the top sheet of paper that was left between the cuts.

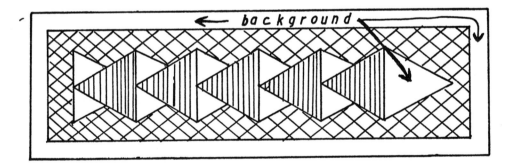

6. Glue the edges of the two strips of paper together.

7. Glue this double piece onto the larger strip of paper, keeping the border as even as possible.

THREE-COLOR BOOKMARK

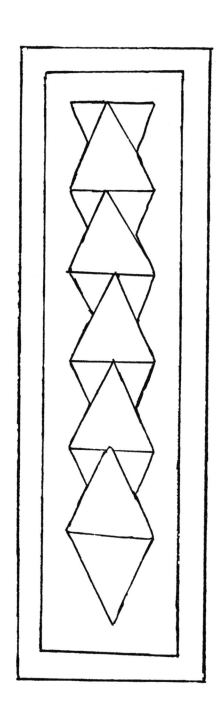

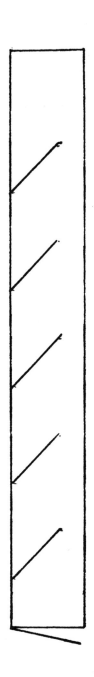

THREE-DIMENSIONAL PICTURE

Objectives: • Learning about dimension
• Using imagination to develop an idea
• Recognizing warm and cool colors

Supplies: Scissors
Glue

Materials: Construction paper for background
Poster or other soft, bendable paper in your choice of warm and cool colors

Directions:

1. Discuss how colors like red, orange, and bright yellow seem warm while blue, green, and white seem cold. Also talk about how flat things, like one piece of paper on top of another, have no depth while something that is thick or loose appears to have a shape. You could also relate this to light and shadow.

2. Distribute the materials and supplies, and suggest that the children cut wide and narrow strips in various lengths. Also suggest using at least one color that is warm and one that is cool.

3. Assemble the pieces on the background. One end might glued in place then twist or fold the paper to give it dimension than glue down the other end. Some may be left loose but curled around a pencil. Others may be folded back and forth in V shapes to show a shadow effect.

4. When the pictures are finished, have a show-and-tell time when children can discuss what they have made and the effect the colors and shapes bring out.

———— TISSUE PICTURE ————

Objectives: • Color recognition
           • Visual alignment (to be able to see how colors overlap and come together to form lines of darker color)
           • Fine motor control

Supplies: Glue
         Fine-tip felt marker, black or purple

Materials: Drawing paper, construction, or poster paper for background, 4½″ × 6″ or 6″ × 9″
          Tissue paper in a variety of colors, about 2″ square

Directions:

1. Discuss colors, making sure that children know all colors. Talk about how colors combine to form other colors. (This will happen when tissue is overlapped.)

2. Distribute supplies and materials.

3. Lay tissue squares around the edges of the background paper, leaving about a 1/4″ margin, keeping the edges as straight as possible, and overlapping the tissue at least 1/2″.

4. Carefully lift the pieces of tissue and tear along all sides that are not next to the border.

5. Glue the edge pieces in place, using only as much glue as necessary to avoid wrinkling.

6. Fill in the rest of the background with smaller pieces of tissue, overlapping in varying amounts. Point out the color changes that happen where colors overlap.

7. When the background is completely covered, set it aside until the glue is dry. While the glue is drying, discuss how the picture will be finished with the markers.

8. A simple, freehand drawing looks best. Some ideas are a flower, a tree, a bird, or perhaps two or three geometric shapes.

Note: You can make a tissue picture greeting card by using 9″ × 12″ paper folded lengthwise, then crosswise, and putting the tissue and picture on the front.

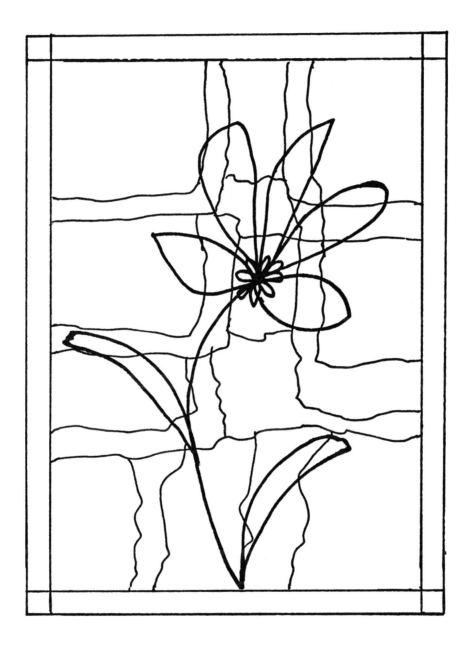

———— TREES ————

Trees are a good subject for projects throughout the year. The following are a few suggestions to get you started.

Objectives: • Understanding changes in the seasons
              • Better observation of nature
              • Symmetry and balance
              • Visual perception
              • Motor control

Supplies: Small branches from trees or bushes
Paper tubes or doweling
Scissors
Pencils
Glue
Thread
Plastic paint pans or styrofoam cups
Plaster of Paris or self-hardening clay or clay made from one of the recipes in this book
Poster paint or food coloring
Newspapers
Wheat paste or wallpaper paste

Materials: Patterns to suit project
Poster paper or other material suitable to project
Crepe paper, brown and/or green
Tissue paper, if appropriate for project

Directions:

1. Choose the supplies that you will need for your particular project. For a seasonal tree to be used more than once, follow the steps listed here.

2. Distribute small branches, or display a large branch if this is to be a group project.

3. Prepare plaster of Paris, clay, or clay dough.

4. Using either a plastic paint pan (metal will not release) or a plastic cup, fill it with the prepared mixture and set the "tree" in the center. Prop or hold until it will stand alone. Set aside to finish hardening.

5. While the base is setting, prepare the leaves or other decorations you plan to use on the tree.

6. For an autumn tree, cut leaves from poster paper or, if it is to be an aspen tree, use tissue paper so the leaves will move in the air.

7. Glue the leaves by their stems to the branches of the tree.

8. At Halloween, either replace the leaves or add among them black and orange Halloween figures cut from paper. They may be glued or hung by threads.

9. For a harvest or Thanksgiving tree, decorate with fruits and/or vegetables or Pilgrims, Indians, etc.

10. At Christmas or Hanukkah, decorate with the usual figures for the season.

11. For Valentine's Day, decorate with hearts and/or flowers.

12. For Easter, decorate with flowers, eggs, and bunnies.

13. Use your imagination to keep your trees exciting all year.

Note: If real tree branches are not available, trees may be made in several other ways:
- Dowling can be secured in a plaster or clay base and rolled paper branches glued onto it.
- Paper tubes make interesting trees. Use papier-mâché or clay dough to enlarge the bottom of the tube so the tree will stand up. Add branches with papier-mâché, rolled paper, or small dowels in holes in the tube.
- If there is a shortage of materials to make a three-dimensional tree, make a tree picture. Small pictures are nice to take home, or make a large one for a bulletin board where it can be decorated.
- Quilling can be used to make a tree or to make things to trim the other types of trees.

There are a number of poems about trees that you can use to motivate tree making. The children can also write poems or stories about trees or conduct a library research project about trees. In addition, the class can take a field trip to observe the trees in your area.

──── WHERE I LIVE ────

Objectives: • Learning directions
               • Using visual and verbal skills to describe
               • Figure-ground discrimination
               • Better understanding of the world around us

Supplies: Pencils
              Crayons or colored pencils (optional)
              Ruler
              Scissors (optional)
              Glue (optional)

Materials: Construction, poster, or drawing paper, 9″ × 12″
               Small pieces of colored paper (optional)

Directions:

1. Discuss with the children how to give directions and how to follow directions. You may also mention using landmarks, and what to do if you feel or know that you are lost.

2. Distribute materials and supplies. Begin by drawing a map with a direction indicator in one corner. Show where the school is and where the child lives. If the distance is too far to show easily on paper, do not draw all the details of streets; rather make a notation such as four blocks showing the direction.

3. If desired, the map can show the school and the child's house as buildings with dimension. Indicate the streets between them.

4. Depending on how the locations are shown, color the picture or add cut-outs of the buildings.

5. When all maps are completed, have each child tell the class how to go from the school to his or her house. In this way, you combine visual and verbal expression in learning to follow a map or direction.

——— WIND SOCK ———

Objectives: • Awareness of direction indicated by the wind
• Following instructions to achieve spacing
• Hand-eye coordination

Supplies: Pencils
Rulers
Glue
Scissors (optional)
Stapler
Paper punch
Crayons, colored pencils, or felt-tip pens (optional)

Materials: Construction paper or tagboard, 3″ × 9″
Tissue paper 12″ × 15″ long, to make strips approximately 1″ wide (variety of colors)

Directions:

1. Discuss wind direction and determine if the children know directions.

2. Distribute supplies and materials. Using the 9″ × 12″ material, measure one long side to determine how many strips will be needed if they are 1″ wide, and 1/8″ to 1/4″ space is left between the strips, with a 1/2″ overlap to join the ends of the paper or tagboard. For younger children, you may have to provide a piece of scrap paper and let them fold it to determine the number of tissue strips needed.

3. Cut the tissue paper into 1″ strips (if this was not done ahead of time). This will require measuring. Unless the strips are fairly straight, they will not move easily.

4. Using the spacing determined in step 2, lay the tissue strips in place, and when they are fairly even, glue in place.

5. Roll the wide strip of paper into a tube shape with the overlap provided, and staple in place.

6. Punch two or four holes in from the top edge, tie a string across, and attach a longer string to hang the wind sock where it will catch a breeze.

7. If you are using tagboard instead of paper, the children may want to draw designs on it before attaching the tissue and finishing the project.

WIND SOCK

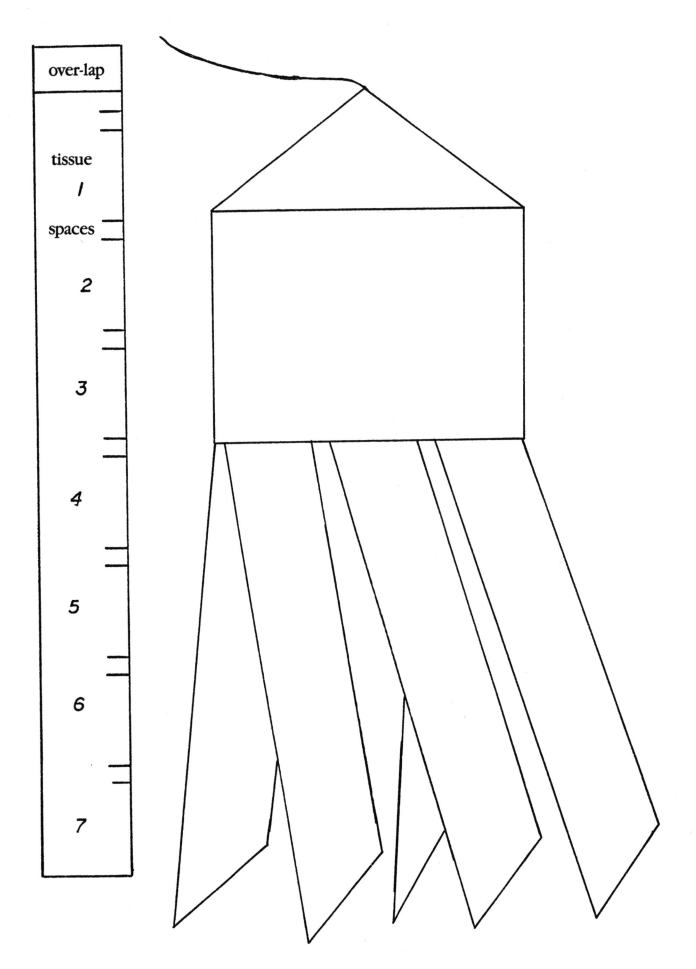

over-lap

tissue

1

spaces

2

3

4

5

6

7

——— WOVEN FISH MOBILE ———

Objectives: • Fine motor dexterity
               • Learning about balance
               • Recognizing angles that give shape

Supplies: Pencils
               Scissors
               Rulers, if measuring
               Colored pencils or felt-tip markers
               Dowels or tightly rolled paper, 10″ long
               Needle

Materials: Construction paper or card stock, four strips 1″ × 3″ paper, two strips 1″ × 4″, or longer strips that can be measured to these lengths, colors of your choice
               Thread or very fine string for hanging

Directions:

1. Distribute the materials and, if measuring, do so.

2. Weave the four shorter strips together, gluing a corner to hold them in place.

3. Add the longer strips and glue the ends to keep the fish from coming apart.

4. Cut the ends of the longer strips on an angle to form the tail of the fish.

5. Using a pencil or marker, make an eye on both sides of the fish, on the corner square opposite the tail.

6. Using the needle and thread, fasten a length of thread to the top of each fish. Leave the thread long enough to make adjustments.

7. Fasten the threads to the dowels or rolled paper so that the fish are at different heights and well balanced. Three to five fish works best.

WOVEN FISH MOBILE

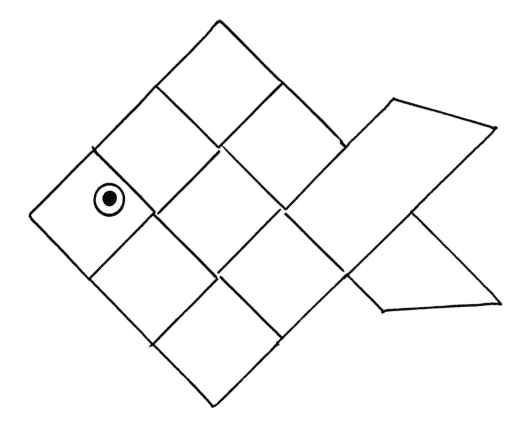

❖❖ **AUTUMN** ❖❖

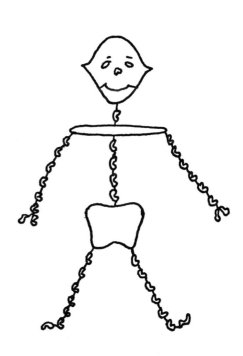

——— CORNUCOPIA ———

Objectives: • Fine motor skills
• Visual perception, figure-ground
• Following directions
• Vocabulary: Cornucopia (horn of plenty), arrangement (objects appear to fall out of the horn); color words: blend, contrast, shades

Supplies: Pencils
Scissors
Glue
Fine-tip felt markers (optional for outlining)

Materials: Construction paper 12″ × 18″, light green or manila for background
Poster paper, dark or medium brown for the cornucopia
Poster paper, light and medium yellow, gold, two shades of red, two shades of green, two shades of orange, tan, purple

Directions:

1. Talk about the picture you are going to make, the meaning of *cornucopia*, and the colors you will use.

2. Distribute materials, and trace all patterns on the colors appropriate for each.

3. Cut out the pieces and glue on leaves where needed. If you are using markers, outline the veins in the leaves, and make appropriate markings on the rest of the pieces.

4. Place the cornucopia on the background and glue in place.

5. Arrange the fruits and vegetables and glue them in place.

Note: Felt-tip markers look best, but if you would rather not use them, use colored pencils or black pencils instead. If you have a small straw cornucopia to show the children, it will help them see how to mark the paper to look like straw.

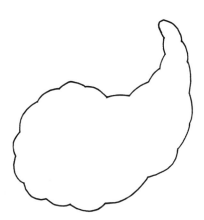

CORNUCOPIA

─── EGG CARTON MASK ───

Objectives: • Eye-hand coordination
              • Motor skills practice
              • Safety in using masks

Supplies: Scissors
           Glue
           Crayons (optional)
           Heavy needle or paper punch
           String or large rubber bands

Materials: Sections of egg cartons
            Paper or yarn scraps for decoration

Directions:

1. Give each child a section of an egg carton consisting of two depressions and one divider.

2. Discuss safety factors to be considered when wearing masks: masks must have large eye holes, they must fit securely so they do not slip and cover eyes, and they must have open space for breathing.

3. Distribute supplies and materials.

4. Cut out the bottom of each depression for eye holes. The divider is the nose of the mask.

5. Using whatever other materials are desired, trim the mask by adding such things as whiskers, hair, or ears.

6. Using the heavy needle or paper punch, make holes on the sides. Fasten string to the holes, or loop a large rubber band in each. The mask can either be tied with the string, or the rubber bands may be looped over the ears.

7. The children will use their imagination in making the masks, but if they need ideas, suggest animals, space creatures, monsters, or storybook characters.

—————— HALF-CIRCLE TURKEY ——————

Objectives: • Shape recognition
• Fine motor control
• Understanding of symmetrical arrangement

Supplies: Scissors
Pencils
Fine-tip felt pen, black
Colored pencil, orange

Materials: Patterns
Manila paper, 9″ square for background
Poster paper, black, 4″ × 7½″, background for tail feathers
Poster paper, orange 2″ × 3½″ for head and feet
Poster paper, light tan, 3″ square for body
Poster paper, light brown, 6″ square for wings and four tail feathers
Poster paper, medium brown, 6″ square for four tail feathers

Directions:

1. Talk about symmetry or balance, and shape—half circle and rounded ends.

2. Distribute materials and have the children trace and cut a 9″ circle from the manila background paper. Set it aside.

3. Trace and cut the background for the feathers from the black paper.

4. Trace and cut the body from the 3″ square. Set it aside.

5. Trace and cut out the feathers, head, wings, and feet.

6. Using the orange pencil, mark the wings.

7. Using the felt-tip pen or a pencil, make loops to indicate feathers on the body. Also make the eyes, wattle, and outline of the bottom of the head/neck.

8. Using the felt-tip pen, outline and mark in two curved wing feathers.

9. Space the feathers, alternating the two colors, on the background. Glue in place.

10. Assemble the head and wings on the body.

11. Glue the feet onto the back of the body.

12. Place the assembled body over the tail feathers and glue in place.

13. Glue the completed turkey onto the manila circle.

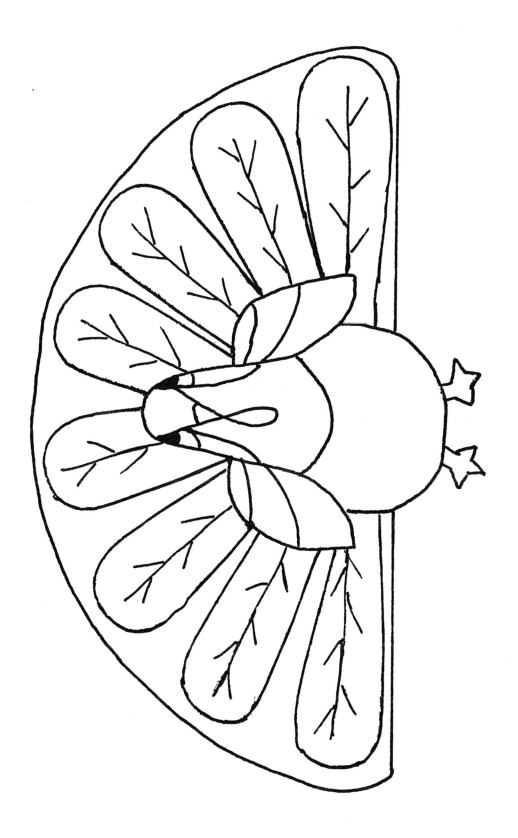

HALF-CIRCLE TURKEY

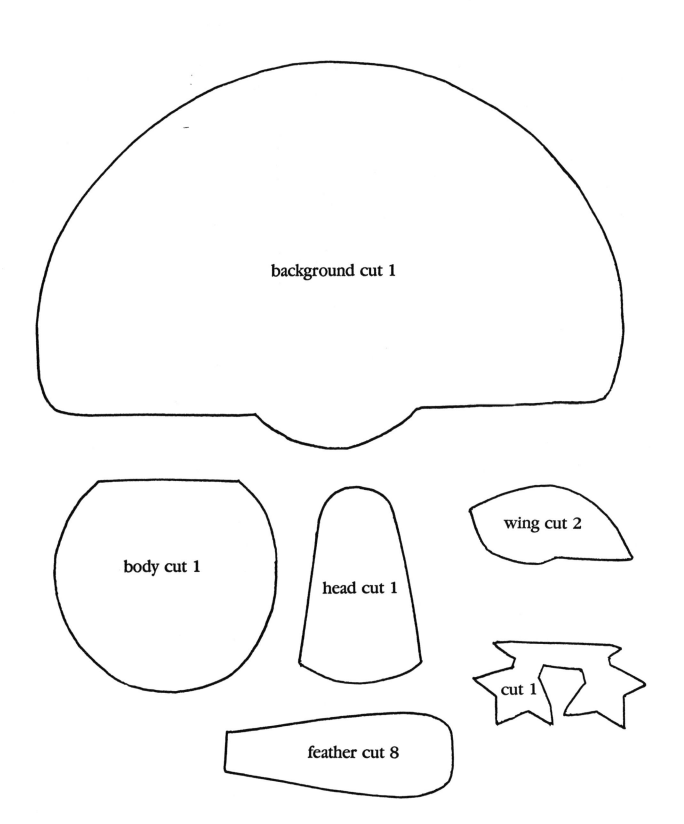

background cut 1

body cut 1

head cut 1

wing cut 2

cut 1

feather cut 8

—— HARVEST PLATES ——

Objectives: • Vocabulary: harvest, kinds of vegetables (root, stalks, vines)
  • Color choices, and detail for recognizable fruits and vegetables
  • Fine motor control

Supplies: Pencils
  Scissors
  Felt-tip pens, matching or contrasting color of paper
  Glue

Materials: Construction paper, any color, 9″ square
  Poster paper:
  Purple, 4″ × 3¼″ (grapes)
  Dark green, 2″ × 1½″ (grape leaf), or 4″ × 4″ for all the leaves
  Gold, 7″ × 2½″ (banana)
  Yellow, 2″ × 2½″ (lemon)
  Red, 2½″ × 2½″ (apple)
  Brown, 3¾″ × 2½″ (potato)
  Orange, 5½″ × 1½″ (carrot)
  Red, 3¼″ × 2½″ (tomato)
  Orange, 2½″ × 2½″ (orange)
  Yellow or white, 4″ × 1″ (corn kernels)
  Green, 5″ × 1½″ (corn husk)
  Yellow, 3″ × 2¼″ (pear)
  Green, 3½″ × 2½″ (pepper)
  Patterns

Directions:

1. Talk about the vocabulary words.

2. Trace and cut a 9″ circle from construction paper for the plate.

3. Choose the fruits or vegetables that you want to use. A good way is to make one plate for fruits and another plate for vegetables.

4. Trace and cut out the pieces you have chosen.

5. Add details with the felt-tip pen. (Do this on a piece of scrap paper if you are tracing around the edges to highlight the shapes.)

6. Arrange the pieces on the plate and glue in place.

HARVEST FRUIT PLATE

———— JACK-O'-LANTERN MOBILE ————

Objectives:
- Eye-hand coordination
- Fine motor control
- Seeing spatial relations and symmetry
- Following directions

Supplies:
Pencils
Scissors
Glue
Patterns
Needle and thread

Materials:
Construction paper, orange 9″ × 12″
Poster paper, black, 6″ square
Poster paper, light brown, 2″ square

Directions:

1. Distribute materials and patterns. Trace pumpkin pattern near one end of the orange paper.

2. Trace the patterns for two sets of small eyes, nose, and mouth on remaining orange paper.

3. Trace the large patterns for eyes, nose, and mouth on the black paper.

4. Trace the stem on the light brown paper; make two.

5. Cut out all the pieces.

6. Glue the small features to both sides of the large black features.

7. Glue stems on each side of the stem of the pumpkin.

8. Use the needle to attach threads to the feature pieces. Leave the thread long; it can be cut off later.

9. Attach the features inside the open space of the pumpkin.

10. Tie another thread through the stem with which to hang the mobile.

Note: If the cut-out part of the pumpkin has been punched and cut out carefully, it can be used to make a "round thing" (See "ROUND THINGS FOR HALLOWEEN" in this section) or as the background for another "round thing," such as an owl or spider.

This might be a good time to talk about Halloween safety in lighting jack-o'-lanterns, such as cutting a small hole in the back and using a flashlight to light the face.

JACK-O'-LANTERN MOBILE

cut 2

cut 1

cut 2

cut 4

cut 2

cut 1

cut 2

cut 1

© 1990 by Parker Publishing Company, Inc.

———— MAYFLOWER ————

Objectives: • Visual closure
• Fine motor skills
• Sequencing parts to a whole

Supplies: Pencils
Scissors
Ruler
Glue

Materials: Ditto sheet of the ship on poster paper, 9″ × 12″, gray-blue or color of your choice
Poster paper, dark blue, 3″ × 9″
Ditto sheet of the hull of the ship on poster paper, dark gray
Manila paper 5½″ × 7″
Patterns for sails

Directions:

1. Distribute the materials. Have the children tear a narrow strip from one of the long sides of the dark blue paper. The remaining strip should be 2¼″ to 2½″ wide.

2. Glue this strip of paper onto the background at the water line.

3. Cut out and glue the hull over the blue water, following and duplicated outline.

4. Trace and cut the sails from the manila paper.

5. Glue the sails in place, following the sketch, starting at the bottom with the largest sail.

6. Using a ruler, trace the rigging and other lines on the ship.

7. If you want to print MAYFLOWER on the banner, have the children practice on another piece of paper to be sure it will fit in the space.

Note: If this project is to be used with a social studies lesson, you might want to include some vocabulary and/or spelling and written work. Some children might like to do a bit of research for details, such as how many children were on board the Mayflower, how many people started the trip, and how many survived.

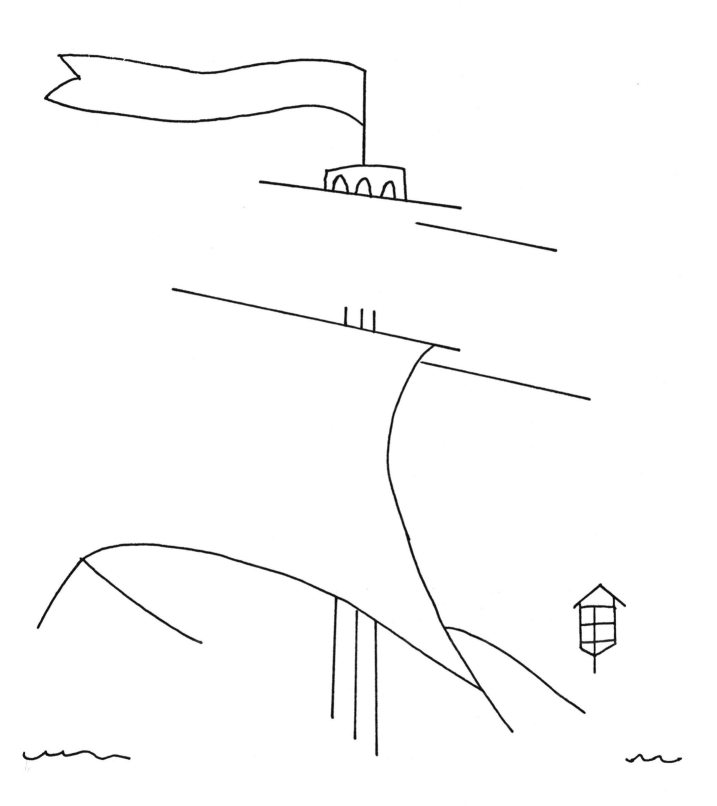

MAYFLOWER

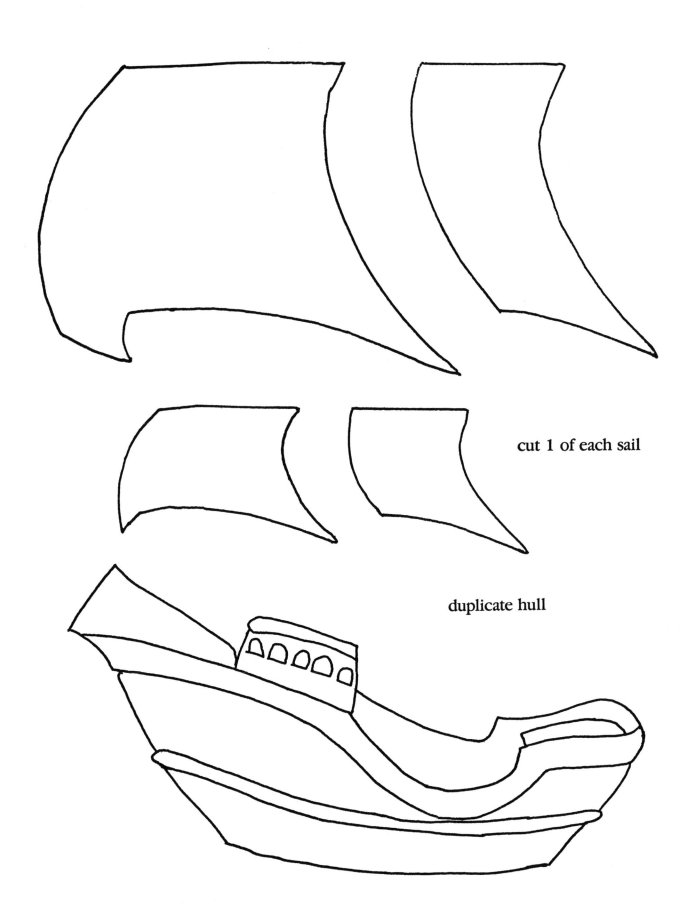

cut 1 of each sail

duplicate hull

──── ROUND THINGS FOR HALLOWEEN ────

Objectives: • Relating shape to familiar objects
• Eye-hand coordination
• Figure-ground and spatial relations
• Following directions

Supplies: Pencils
Scissors
Glue
Crayons

Materials: Poster paper in colors and sizes appropriate for project
Circle patterns 4″ to 8″ in diameter

Directions:

1. Talk about familiar things that are round. Talk about Halloween in terms of shapes and colors.

2. Distribute materials and have children trace and cut out circles to make cats, owls, jack-o'-lanterns, or other figures.

3. Add features using scraps of paper or crayons.

———— SEGMENTED LEAVES ————

Objectives: • Eye-hand coordination
  • Closure, parts to a whole
  • Organization and balance
  • Vocabulary: background, color contrasting or blending, position, and spacing

Supplies: Pencils
  Scissors
  Glue

Materials: Poster or construction paper, neutral color for the background, 8″ square for each leaf
  Poster paper in autumn colors, 7″ square for each leaf
  Newsprint (optional, for practice in cutting sections)
  Patterns or leaves

Directions:

1. Talk about why some colors are called autumn colors. Talk about the effect of colors that contrast or blend. Discuss arrangement, position, and spacing in organizing the sections of the cut leaves.

2. Distribute materials, trace leaves or patterns on newsprint or poster paper, and cut out.

3. If using the newsprint for practice, draw lines with pencil where cuts will be made. Use a maximum of three cuts to make four sections. Spread apart to see if the balance is good.

4. When finished practicing, trace and cut the leaves from the colored paper.

5. Cut the leaf apart and arrange the pieces on the background paper, leaving about 1/4″ space between segments.

6. Glue the pieces in place.

SKELETON

Objectives: • Learn body parts: arms, legs, clavicle, pelvis
• Fine motor control

Supplies: Pencils
Scissors
Large needle
Black crayon

Materials: Styrofoam tray (such as trays used to package produce)
Styrofoam packing (long pieces rather than round)
Lightweight string
Patterns

Directions:

1. Discuss body parts as related to bone structure. Emphasize that the bones are a framework to hold the body together.

2. Distribute materials and have the children trace patterns on the styrofoam and cut them out.

3. Using the black crayon, draw features on the skull.

4. Using a piece of string about 15″ long, thread the needle and tie a knot in the other end of the string.

5. Tie or fasten the string to the skeleton's chin; then push the needle through one of the packing pieces, lengthwise, for the neck.

6. Push the needle through the center of the clavicle and add four pieces of packing for the backbone.

7. Fasten the string to the center of the wide side of the pelvis by tying it. Cut off any extra string.

8. Using another piece of string, push the needle through one end of the clavicle and add six packing pieces for an arm.

9. Push the needle through the ends of two packing pieces for a hand. Tie a knot in the string.

10. Repeat steps 8 and 9 on the other side for the second arm and hand.

11. Tie or fasten another piece of string to one side of the narrow part of the pelvis.

12. String seven pieces of packing for a leg. Fasten another piece of packing, tightly, at the end to represent a foot.

13. Repeat steps 11 and 12 for the second leg.

14. Thread a piece of string at the top of the skull to hang up the skeleton.

Note: The length of the strings will depend on the length of the packing pieces. To avoid tangling, do not make the strings much longer than necessary. These skeletons will move with the slightest air current.

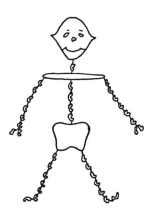

SKELETON

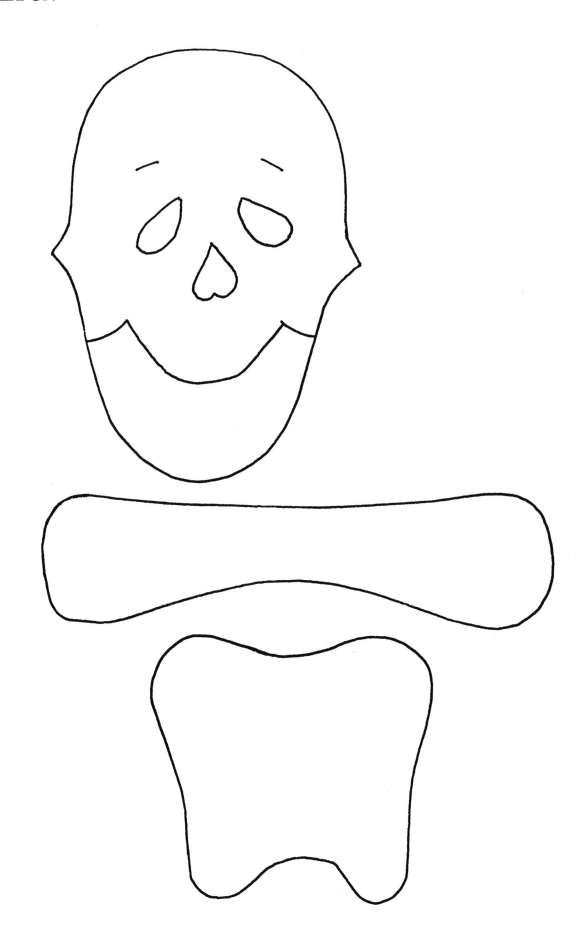

SQUARE BLACK CAT

Objectives:
- Recognition of the square shape in objects
- Eye-hand coordination
- Following directions

Supplies: Scissors
  Glue
  Yellow crayon

Materials: Poster paper, black 9″ square

Directions:

1. Talk about things we see around us that are square. Ask what shape is seen in half a square.

2. Distribute materials and have the children fold the square to form a rectangle.

3. Cut a narrow rectangle out of the center of both of the open sides (found opposite the folded side). Set one of the pieces aside to use later.

4. Fold the other rectangle into a square and, following the diagram, cut one open side to form the ears of the cat.

5. Unfold the rectangle and glue the head to one corner of the body on the folded side.

6. Use the other rectangular piece to cut a curved tail.

7. Glue the tail inside the fold opposite the head.

8. Using the yellow crayon, give the cat a pair of slanted eyes.

9. Spread the open side slightly apart, and the cat will stand up.

Note: If you would like to use this lesson as an exercise in measuring, the children can measure and draw the part to be cut out to form the legs of the cat. They can also measure and draw the lines where they will cut to form the ears. They might like to try attaching the head in the center of the fold and letting the tail hang down as though the cat is sitting on a fence.

The children might imagine other animals that can fit into a square shape, not necessarily for Halloween. Let them try their ideas.

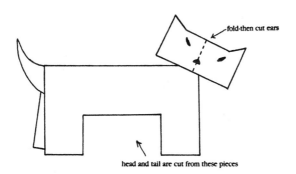

fold-then cut ears

head and tail are cut from these pieces

THANKSGIVING PLACEMAT

Just a reminder in regard to the cinquain. It consists of five lines: line 1, one word that names the subject; line 2, two words that describe the subject; line 3, three words that show action associated with the subject; line 4, four words that express feeling about the subject; line 5, one word that sums up, or is a synonym for, the subject.

Example:

puppy

soft, cuddly

playful, wiggly, sleepy

we love our puppy

happy

If you are working with young children who tend to write very large, you may want to write the cinquain ahead of time and type it so that it will fit on the plate. The children can glue it on when the plate has been decorated.

Objectives: • Vocabulary: over/under, cinquain, lengthwise, design
 • Organization and sequencing of materials
 • Combining a paper project with a written lesson

Supplies: Pencils
 Scissors
 Crayons, colored pencils, or fine-tip felt pens
 Glue

Materials: Poster paper, any color, 9″ × 12″
 Poster paper, seven strips 1″ × 12″, in harmonizing or contrasting color
 Poster paper, white or very light color, 7″ or 8″ square
 Poster paper, light gray, 4″ × 8″
 Patterns
 Writing paper for practice

Directions:

1. Talk about the vocabulary words, beginning with *cinquain* and explaining how the words can be used.

2. Using the writing paper, have the children write a cinquain about Thanksgiving, harvest, or another appropriate subject.

3. Distribute the other materials and have the children trace and cut out the circle pattern for a plate.

4. Decorate the edge of the plate, keeping it to about 1/2″ width.

5. Copy the cinquain onto the center of the plate and set aside.

6. Talk about the other vocabulary words. Then have the children fold the 9″ × 12″ paper lengthwise.

7. Cut curved or angled slits from the folded side, stopping about 1/2″ from the open edges.

8. Weave the seven strips of paper through the cut slits. Glue the ends after all are in place and even. Set aside.

9. Trace and cut out the knife, fork, and spoon.

10. Arrange the plate and flatware on the woven placemat and glue them in place.

THANKSGIVING PLACEMAT

TORN PAPER JACK-O'-LANTERN

Objectives:
- Listening and following directions
- Figure-ground discrimination
- Visual motor coordination

Supplies:
Pencils
Glue

Materials:
Construction paper, manila or any light color, 9″ × 12″ for background
Orange poster paper, 6″ × 9″
Poster paper scraps, green or tan, and yellow
Pattern for outline of pumpkin

Directions:

1. Distribute materials and have the children trace the pattern on the background paper.

2. Tear small pieces of green or tan paper and glue them to cover the stem.

3. Tear slightly larger pieces of orange paper and glue them to cover the pumpkin.

4. Tear smaller pieces of yellow paper to fit the spaces and glue them to make features.

Note: If you use construction paper for the torn pieces, it will give a mottled look because the edges will be a lighter color. Remind the children to put the glue on the small pieces, not the background, or the background will either get too wet or will become dry before it is covered.

TORN PAPER JACK-O'-LANTERN

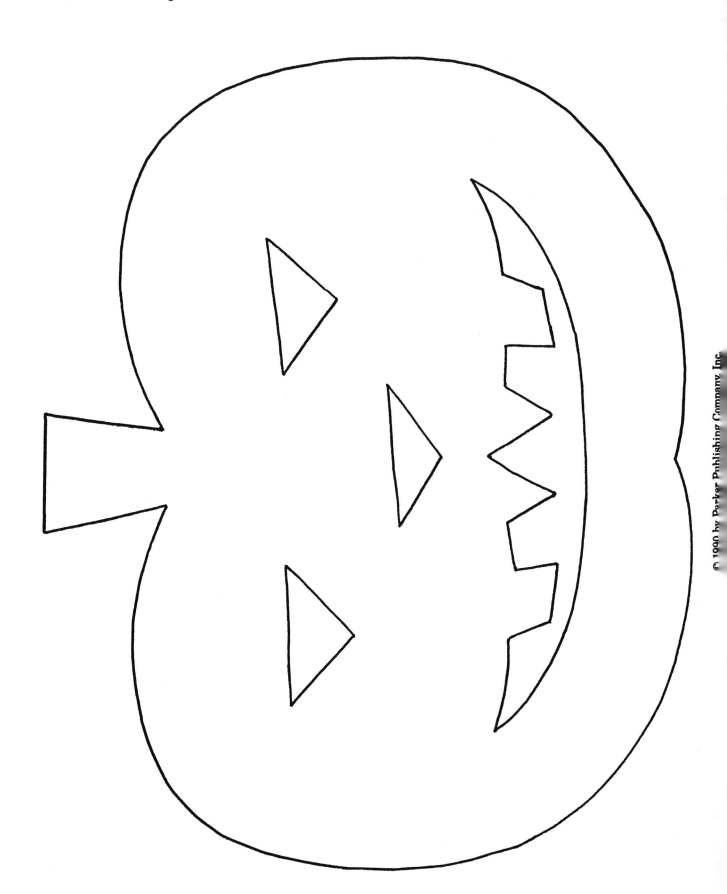

TORN PAPER TURKEY

Objectives: • Reinforce figure-ground recognition
• Fine motor skills

Supplies: Glue
Crayons
Fine-tip felt pen or large, soft lead pencil

Materials: Ditto of a turkey on tagboard or construction paper
Poster paper, brown, 3″ × 12″
Poster paper, scraps of various colors

Directions:

1. Distribute materials and have children use crayons to color the head and chest brown, but not the beak or wattle.

2. Color the beak and feet yellow-orange.

3. Color the wattle red.

4. Make the eye with black crayon, felt-tip pen, or soft lead pencil.

5. Tear brown paper in small pieces and glue them over the body and the wing of the turkey.

6. Draw in the wing outline with felt pen or pencil.

7. Tear the colored paper into small pieces and glue them to cover the tail feathers in a variety of colors.

Note: If you do not care for the fantasy idea of colored tail feathers, the feathers can be the same color as the body of the turkey. Also, if you want to speed up the process, the tail feathers may be torn as single units either in brown or various colors.

The turkeys may be cut out and mounted on a different background, which will give more depth to the picture.

TORN PAPER TURKEY

❖❖ **WINTER** ❖❖

CHRISTMAS GOOSE CARD

For hundreds of years, people celebrated the winter solstice with feasting. The choice of meat changed over time from the ox to the pig, boar, peacock and, finally, the goose. The goose was readily available and became a Christmas tradition in England and Europe.

Objectives:
- Hand-eye coordination
- Fine motor control
- Understanding the goose as a tradition

Supplies:
Pencils
Scissors
Glue or paste

Materials:
Construction paper, medium blue, 9″ × 12″
Poster paper, white, 4″ × 9″
Small piece of poster paper, medium yellow
Patterns for goose, wing, feet, and beak

Directions:

1. Talk with the children about goose being a traditional part of the English Christmas dinner.

2. Distribute supplies and materials.

3. Tell children to set aside the blue paper to use later.

4. Trace and cut out the pieces.

5. Glue the wing, feet, and beak in place on the goose.

6. Fold the blue paper in half to form a card 6″ × 9″.

7. Glue the goose on the front of the card with the fold on the left side.

8. A message may be written on the inside, or a typed verse may be glued in place. Example: The Christmas goose has come to say, "Have a merry Christmas day."

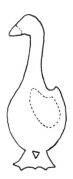

CHRISTMAS GOOSE CARD

CONE ORNAMENT

Objectives: • Sequencing directions
• Fine motor control

Supplies: Scissors
Glue
Thread for hanging

Materials: Tissue paper or thin gift wrap, white for snowballs or colors for ornaments
3″ circle pattern

Directions:

1. Distribute materials. Fold the paper before tracing the pattern so that several circles can be cut at one time.

2. Trace and cut about eighteen circles.

3. Cut each circle to the center.

4. Overlap the edges at the cut to form a cone. The paper is now double. Glue in place by using a tiny bit of glue along the entire edge of the overlap.

5. Glue the sides of the cones together with the points to the center. Begin with six cones in a circle.

6. Fill in the space on each side of the circle with more cones until a ball is formed.

7. Attach a thread for hanging.

Note: Any paper soft enough to roll into a small cone shape will make a pretty ornament. If the cones are rolled too tightly, it will take more than eighteen cones to make a ball without open spaces or irregular shape.

CONE ORNAMENT

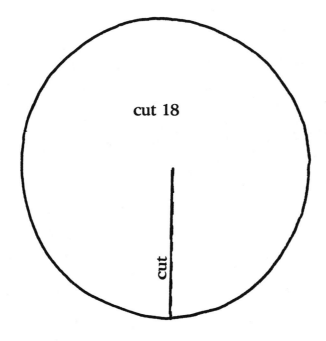

cut 18

cut

Roll circle to form cone

━━━ COOKIE CUTTER ART ━━━

Objectives: • Recognizing multiuse of objects
• Hand-eye coordination
• Figure-ground reinforcement
• Fine motor control

Supplies: Cookie cutters
Pencils
Scissors
Glue (optional)
Crayons or colored pencils (optional)

Materials: Construction or poster paper, 9″ × 12″ for background, color of choice
Poster or construction paper, if making figures from patterns
Patterns, if not using cookie cutters

Directions:

1. Talk with children about using unusual objects for an art project (in this case, cookie cutters).

2. Distribute materials and supplies.

3. If using cookie cutters, have the children trace around them on the background paper. Then color the shapes.

4. If using patterns, choose the ones to be used, trace, and cut out the pieces.

5. On the background paper, arrange the pieces to create a pleasing picture.

Note: When talking to the children about this project, suggest combinations that would make a picture. Limit the number of shapes that can be used, or they will want to include all of them. For example, a winter scene might be two snowmen and one or two trees. Also, decide ahead of time if the figures will be silhouettes or if details will be added with crayons or pencils.

COOKIE CUTTER ART
Shapes from a child's baking set

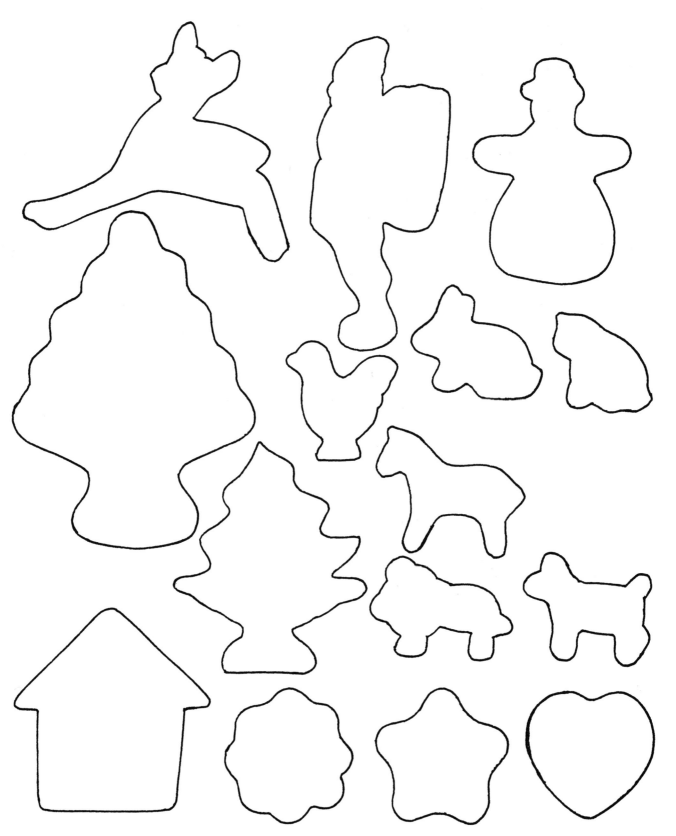

FOLD-AND-CUT VALENTINE

Objectives: • Fine motor control
  • Sequencing
  • Observing rules for proportion and shape
  • Color coordination

Supplies: Scissors
  Glue

Materials: Poster paper, 6″ squares, one each of three colors
  Pattern for half of a large heart

Directions:

1. Set aside one square of paper for the background.

2. Fold the second piece of paper in half and lightly trace the half heart. *Do not cut it out.*

3. With the paper still folded, draw lightly and/or cut from the folded side an irregular continuous shape. One end must be left attached at the fold because this is a double cut taking out an irregular piece from the inside of the heart.

4. Open and place it on the background, but *do not glue* it yet.

5. Fold the third piece of paper and trace and cut out a large heart.

6. Using the piece cut from the second piece of paper as a guide, cut a smaller design from the third heart. Try the pieces together, and cut away any bits that do not let all three colors show.

7. When all three pieces have been shaped to form a pleasing design, glue them together.

FOLD-AND-CUT VALENTINE

——— FOLDED ORNAMENTS ———

Objectives: • Sequencing directions
• Eye-hand coordination

Supplies: Paper cutter
String for hanging

Materials: Paper: poster, gift wrap, foil backed, or any paper that will fold easily; 8″ or larger square for the bell ornament (must be square)
Paper: poster, ribbon, or other paper of your choice for the star; four pieces, one or two colors, 1/2″ × 18″ or 3/4″ × 24″

Directions:

1. The easiest way to form the bell and/or star ornaments is to follow the diagrams.

2. Sometimes it works best to enlarge the diagrams so the children can see them easily as you take them through the folds.

3. The folding seems difficult until you try it, but like origami, it comes easily once you get started. Children catch on quickly and are proud of the finished ornament.

FOLDED BELL

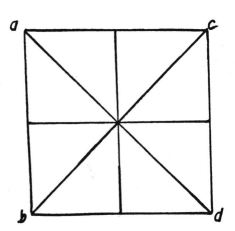

1. Crease a square on diagonal, vertical, and horizontal lines.

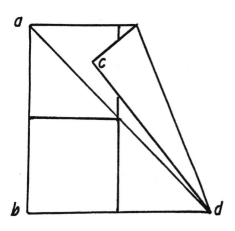

2. Fold corner "c" on diagonal and "b" same diagonal.

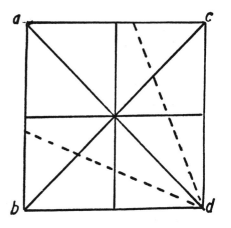

3. Open folds radiating from "d."

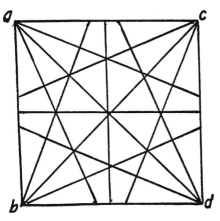

4. Do the same from "a," "b," and "c." It will look like this.

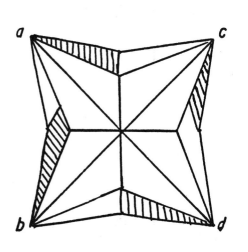

5. Bend the creases so the paper looks like the diagram at the left. Gently pull upward on the four outer points until they meet. Fasten the points.

──────── FOLDED PAPER STAR ────────

The following instructions are numbered in the same order as the diagrams for the folded star. The shaded areas in diagrams 3, 4, 5, and 7 help in following these directions.

Fold each strip in half and cut the ends into tapered points. Snip off the tip to make it a blunt cut.

1. Place four folded strips in interlocking position to form a basket weave. Dotted lines indicate continuation of the strips.

2. Tighten the basket weave until the four strips are firmly interlocked. *Turn over.* Holding in the left hand, turn down front strip at upper left. Crease and turn star clockwise.

3. Fold down three remaining top strips to form a second basket weave, turning clockwise. When you turn down the fourth strip, weave it through the first strip as shown by the shaded area.

4. Fold the upper right strip away from you to make a right-angle triangle 1. Fold the strip toward you to form triangle 2. Fold triangle 2 over triangle 1 to form a flat point as in diagram 5.

5. Weave the end of the paper strip under the woven area as shown. Turn clockwise and make points on three remaining upper right-hand strips. Push loose strip out of your way for the last weaving.

6. *Turn the star over* and repeat steps 4 and 5 until you have eight points. Your star will look like the diagram, four strips showing in back of four points and four strips covering four points.

7. To make the center points, take the end of the lower right-hand strip in right hand and, with a loop motion (shaded area), keeping right-side-up, push through upper left-hand basket weave and flat point.

8. Pull strip tight to form a point. Turn the star clockwise and continue until you have four points at the center. *Turn over* and repeat on the other side. Trim ends. Hang with thread or fine wire.

Note: Exact width and straightness are essential when cutting the strips. The size of the strips may be varied to make different sizes of stars. For a 4″ star, cut the strips 1″ wide and 30″ long. To make a 2½″ star, cut the strips 1/2″ wide and 18″ long. For a 1½″ star, cut the strips 3/8″ wide and 13″ long.

For younger children, you might want to stop after the eight points are formed, eliminating the center points.

FOLDED STAR

Numbers below correspond with numbers on the instruction sheet.

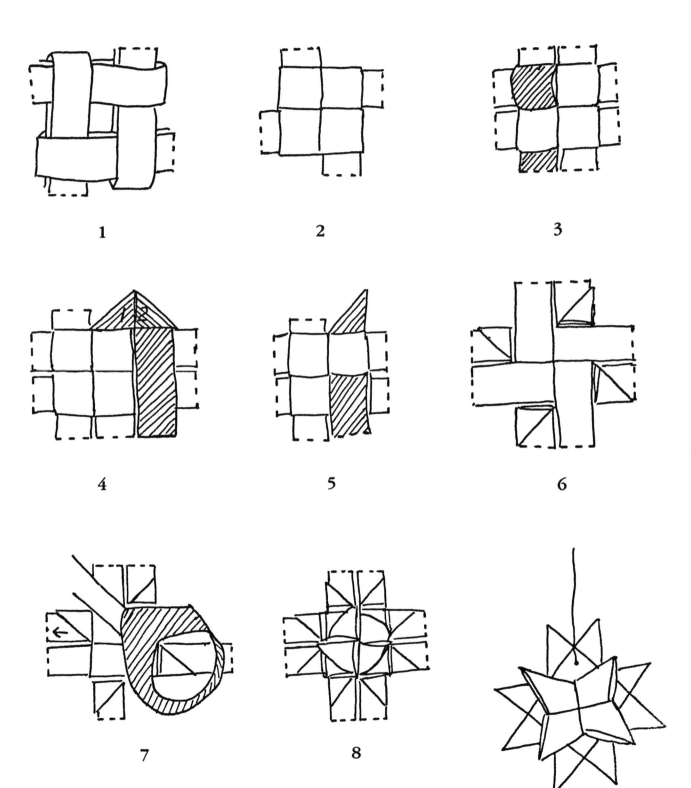

1

2

3

4

5

6

7

8

———— HEART FLOWERS ————

Objectives: • Fine motor control
• Spacial awareness
• Following directions

Supplies: Scissors
Glue
Pencils (optional)

Materials: Poster paper, 6″ square, any light shade for background
Poster paper, 1½″ × 6″, red or pink
Poster paper, 3½″ × 4″, green
Patterns

Directions:

1. Fold the strip of paper in half three times.

2. Draw or trace pattern for half heart on folded edge where the open ends are (the rounded side of the heart on the side where there are folds only).

3. Cut out the hearts. There should be four hearts connected. Set this aside.

4. Cut four stems from the green paper.

5. Using scraps from flowers, cut small hearts for buds.

6. Arrange the pieces on the background with the stems coming over the tips of the heart flowers.

7. Glue all pieces in place.

HEART FLOWERS

———— HEARTS AND FLOWERS VALENTINE ————

Objectives: • Figure-ground discrimination
  • Choosing colors
  • Fine motor control
  • Random placement for special effect
  • Freehand cutting

Supplies: Scissors
  Glue
  Pencils (optional for drawing)

Directions:

1. Talk about random or scattered placement. Show an example of small hearts and flowers randomly placed. Demonstrate by dropping onto a piece of paper.

2. Talk about how many hearts and flowers would make the best-looking picture. Too many will look crowded.

3. Cut or trace and cut out the number of pieces necessary for the card.

4. Arrange the pieces on the background, and when the design pleases you, glue the pieces in place.

──── HOLLY WREATH ────

Objectives: • Fine motor control
• Following directions

Supplies: Scissors
Glue
Paper punch
Lightweight string

Materials: Thin paper plate, or heavy tagboard cut into a circle
Poster paper, one or two harmonizing shades
Poster paper, scraps of red
Crepe paper, red
Holly leaf pattern (optional)

Directions:

1. Cut the center from the paper plate or the tagboard circle.

2. Punch a hole near the outside edge of the circle and attach a string for hanging.

3. Cut freehand or trace and cut out holly leaves a few at a time.

4. Glue the leaves on the paper ring close together or with some overlapping to form a covered wreath.

5. Using the paper punch and red paper, make some berries and glue in groups of two or three.

6. Cut a strip of crepe paper and tie a bow. Glue it to the top of the wreath where the hanger was tied.

Note: Since wreaths are now popular at all times of year, you can replace the holly leaves with autumn leaves, flowers, or any other items appropriate to the season or use.

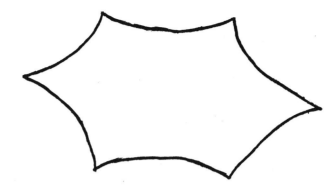

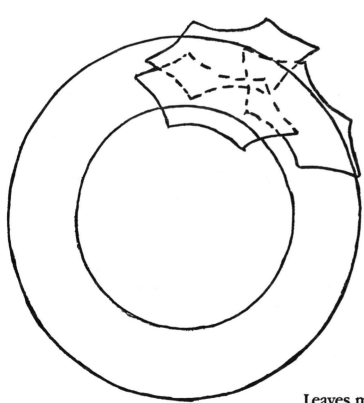

Leaves must overlap, but stay within the circle.

MOLA OR LAYERED VALENTINE

This project is a simplified form of the art developed in the 1890s by the Cuna Indian women of Eastern Panama. Cloth traders offered a variety of colors that the women used to appliqué bands on skirt hems. Through a series of changes, the process was expanded to include a whole dress. More layers of cloth, more elaborate patterns, and the addition of beads, shells, and sometimes mirror fragments were added. During the 1960s, the Peace Corps went to San Blas (an area of Panama), and the outside world became aware of this art form. (A reference is *Molas* by Rhoda L. Auld, published by Van Nostrand Reinhold.)

Objectives: • Vocabulary: mola, layered, off center or irregular
           • Following directions and sequencing
           • Color coordination

Supplies: Pencils
            Scissors
            Glue

Materials: Poster paper in three colors, at least 6″ square
            Newsprint or other drawing paper, same size, for sketching pattern ideas

Directions:

1. Talk about the vocabulary words.

2. Let the children choose three pieces of paper. Set them aside.

3. Using the newsprint, sketch ideas for an irregularly shaped heart. Then draw other hearts inside, being careful to use double lines so they can be cut out later. Children should try to design the heart so there will be two spaces for each color.

4. Using letters for the colors of paper to be used, label the drawing. (r = red, p = pink, pr = purple)

5. Using the newsprint sketch as a guide, begin cutting the shapes. Be careful that you do not spoil paper you will need for other parts of the design.

6. Put the layers together and trim, if necessary, to get the desired look. Then glue in place.

Note: A fourth color of paper can be used for a background and will only show in the very center of the design. Also, a similar design may be made by cutting shapes and gluing in layers on the background, but this does not give a real mola look.

———— PAPER CHAINS ————

Objectives: • Fine motor coordination
      • Sequencing directions

Supplies: Scissors
      Glue
      Pencils

Materials: Poster paper (any appropriate colors)
      Pattern for small or large chain

Directions:

1. Distribute materials and have children trace and cut out several rings using one or two colors.

2. Put a drop of glue on opposite sides of one ring.

3. Place a second ring on top of the first and press down.

4. Turn the rings 90° and place a drop of glue on opposite sides of the top of the second ring.

5. Continue turning and gluing until there is a nice stack of rings. When the glue is dry, rings will pull out into an attractive chain.

Note: If there is a question about the accuracy of the turning and gluing, try just a few rings. If the rings don't separate into a chain, the glue is not in the right place. If it is easier for the children, tell them to glue on the sides the first time, then on the top and bottom, and alternate. The glue must be at right angles, or you will have just a stack of rings glued together.

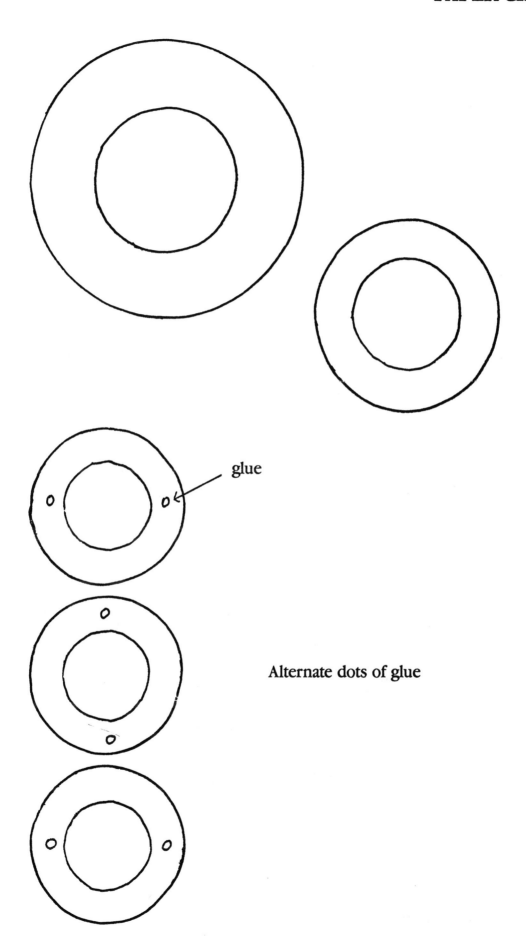

glue

Alternate dots of glue

——————— PAPIER-MÂCHÉ SNOW PEOPLE ———————

Objectives: • Visual motor control
   • Learning concept of size
   • Delayed gratification

Supplies: Wheat paste and container for mixing
   Pencils
   Scissors
   Glue

Materials: Old newspapers
   White paper towels
   Poster or construction paper, black or other colors
   Waxed paper

Directions:

1. Distribute old newspapers and begin crumpling into a ball shape. Add paper until there are enough of the right-size balls to make a snowman/snowwoman. Be sure the paper is wadded tightly as if making real snowballs.

2. Tear paper towels into strips about 2″ wide.

3. Using the wheat paste, glue the paper towel strips over the newspaper until the balls are completely covered and no black is showing through.

4. Place the balls on waxed paper and let them dry. The time to dry will depend on how large the balls are and how much paste was used.

5. When the balls are dry, glue on features using black or other colors of paper.

6. To fasten the balls together, use either the wheat paste or other paper glue. If a flat place can't be found, they may need to be propped in position.

Note: Other things can be added to the snow people, such as hats, collars, or even big feet. For a hat, measure the diameter of the head and draw a circle that size. Draw another circle around it the width you would like the brim to be. To make the crown of the hat, use the diameter measurement and add enough for an overlap to glue into a tube. Measure the height of the crown and add 2″. Cut in 1″ on both the top and bottom of the tube, making tabs that can be folded in on the top and out at the bottom and glued to the brim and the top. Cut a circle for the top of the crown. Now glue the pieces together. You will probably want a second brim for the bottom, to cover the tabs where the crown was glued to the brim.

PLEATED SNOWFLAKE

Objectives: • Fine motor control
• Listening and following directions

Supplies: Scissors
Stapler
Glue

Materials: Tissue paper, white or pastel colors, 3″ × 20″, or poster paper 4″ × 12″
Thread for hanging

Directions:

1. Distribute materials and be sure children know how to fold as if making a fan.

2. Beginning at the short end of the paper, fold fan-like about 1/2″ wide.

3. If using tissue paper, staple near one end of the folded stack.

4. If using poster paper, staple in the center of the folded stack.

5. Cut out small pieces along folded edges and/or on the ends of the folds to give a lacy look.

6. Unfold and glue the open ends to form a circle.

7. Attach thread for hanging.

Note: If these are made of brightly colored tissue or poster paper, they may be used as flowers. Instead of cutting small pieces from the folded sides, cut in flower shapes, making sure not to cut out too much of the folded sides.

━━━━━ ROCKING HORSE OR REINDEER ━━━━━

Objectives: • Observing changes in shape
              • Fine and visual motor coordination
              • Following directions

Supplies: Pencils
         Scissors
         Glue

Materials: Construction or poster paper: yellow, tan, or other light color of your choice, 7″ or 8″ square
         Patterns: 6″ circle and pattern for cutting
         Scraps of yarn for tail

Directions:

1. Distribute materials and have children trace and cut out the 6″ circle.

2. Fold the circle in half and trace the cutting pattern on it.

3. Cut on the line a to b to c.

4. Pull up the cut strip and reverse the fold. Crease it at an angle into the larger part of the circle. This fold forms the neck.

5. Reverse the fold back to the original position on the end of the neck, folding on an angle to form the head.

6. Round the end of the head for a nose.

7. Using scraps of paper, cut ears for the horse or ears and antlers for the reindeer. Glue in place.

8. Cut about five 2″ lengths of yarn for a tail and glue inside the top folded edge.

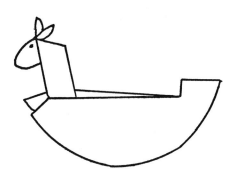

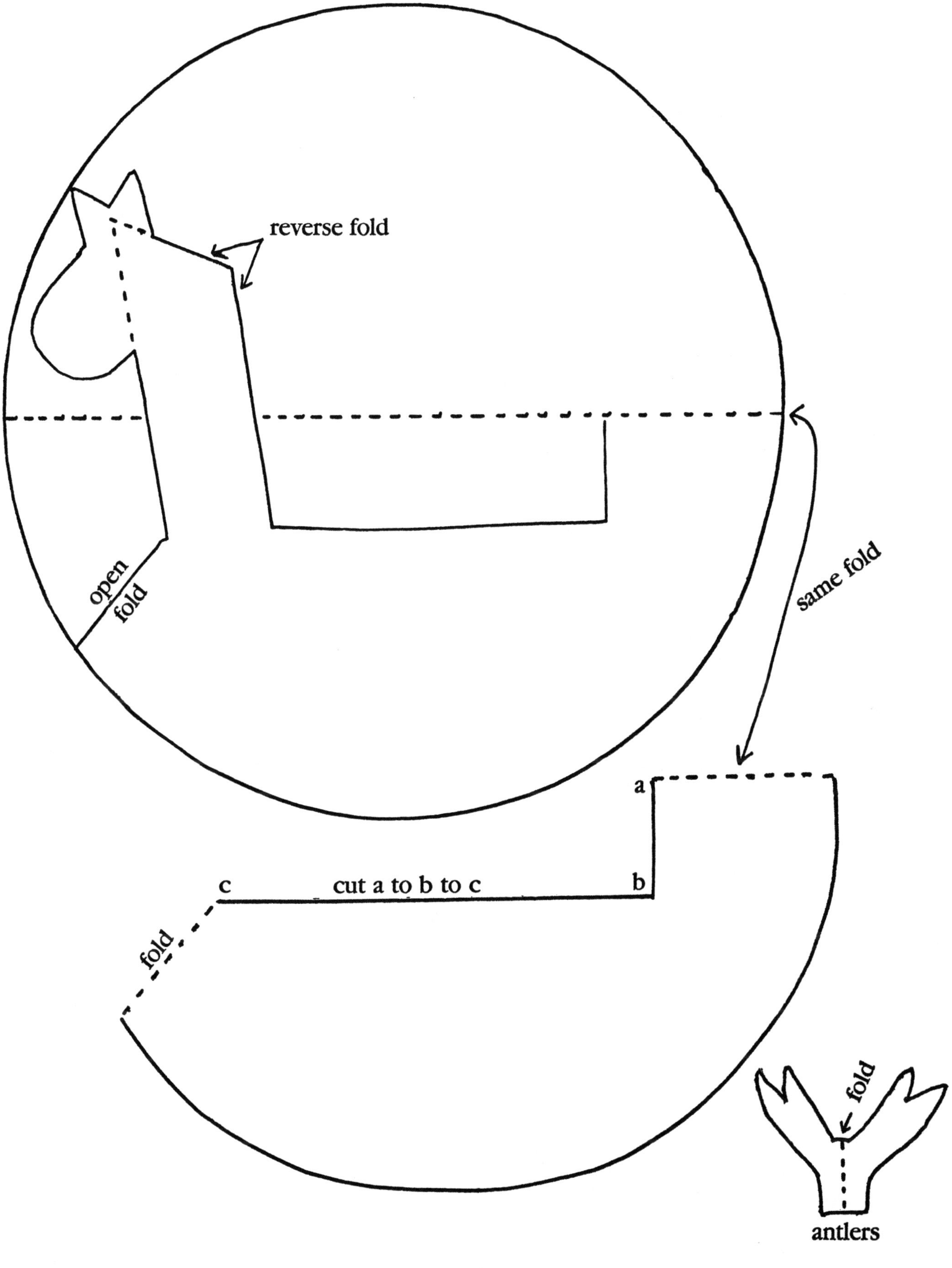

ROCKING HORSE

© 1990 by Parker Publishing Company, Inc.

reverse fold

open fold

same fold

a

c   cut a to b to c   b

fold

fold

antlers

─── ROSE ───

This rose can be used as a Mother's Day corsage, for Christmas, or for a valentine. It can be used as a spring flower or with leaves on a twisted crepe paper vine as part of a bulletin board display.

Objectives:
- Visual motor coordination
- Sequencing actions and directions
- Using a ruler

Supplies:
Scissors
Florist wire or twist ties (green, if possible)
Pencils
Rulers

Materials:
Tissue paper—about 5″ × 14″, color appropriate for a flower
Green crepe paper, 1″ × 8″

Directions:

1. Measure and cut a 3″ square and a 4″ square from the tissue paper.

2. Crush the 3″ square into a ball.

3. Place the ball in the center of the 4″ square and wrap the ball to look like a flower bud. Secure the base with wire. Set this aside.

4. Trace and cut out seven petals.

5. Place the petals around the bud, one at a time, keeping the straight sides (bottom of the petal) even with each other.

6. Wrap another wire around the petals to hold them together around the center, leaving about a 2″ stem, if possible.

7. Wrap the base of the flower and the double stem with the crepe paper strip. Wrap in a spiral.

Note: By attaching the flower to a star made by covering cardboard with silver paper, you can make an attractive Christmas ornament.

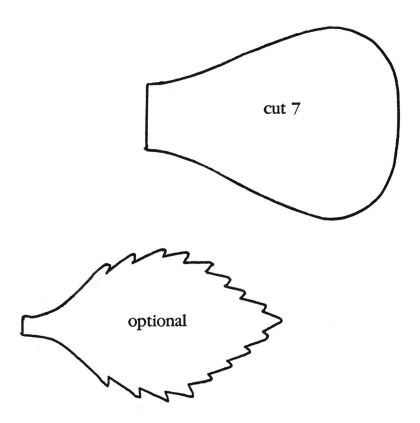

cut 7

optional

SANTA MOBILE

Objectives: • Fitting parts to a whole
           • Fine motor control
           • Visual motor integration

Supplies: Pencil
           Scissor
           Needle and lightweight thread

Materials: Construction paper, red 9″ square
           Construction paper, white 4″ or 5″ square
           Construction paper, black—small pieces
           Patterns

Directions:

1. Distribute supplies and materials.

2. Using the pattern and red paper, trace and cut out the ring. From the center piece trace and cut two small circles.

3. Using the white paper and patterns, trace and cut out whiskers and eyebrows.

4. From the black paper, trace and cut out two small circles.

5. To assemble, lay out the pieces inside the red ring. The whiskers should be over the bottom of the ring.

6. Fasten the knot of a piece of thread about 10″ long to one side of a small red circle. Hold the circle just inside the whiskers, then pull the needle through the back of the whiskers, up and through from the front to the back.

7. Thread the other circle onto this thread for the nose. Run the thread over and under the ring, but do not fasten it yet.

8. Fasten a thread to one side of a black circle; then using an under-over thread connect it with a white eyebrow. Then connect it to the ring about 1½″ to 1¾″ from the thread put in first.

9. Connect the other eye and eyebrow in the same way.

10. When all pieces appear to be in balance, tie each of the three threads at the top of the ring.

SANTA MOBILE

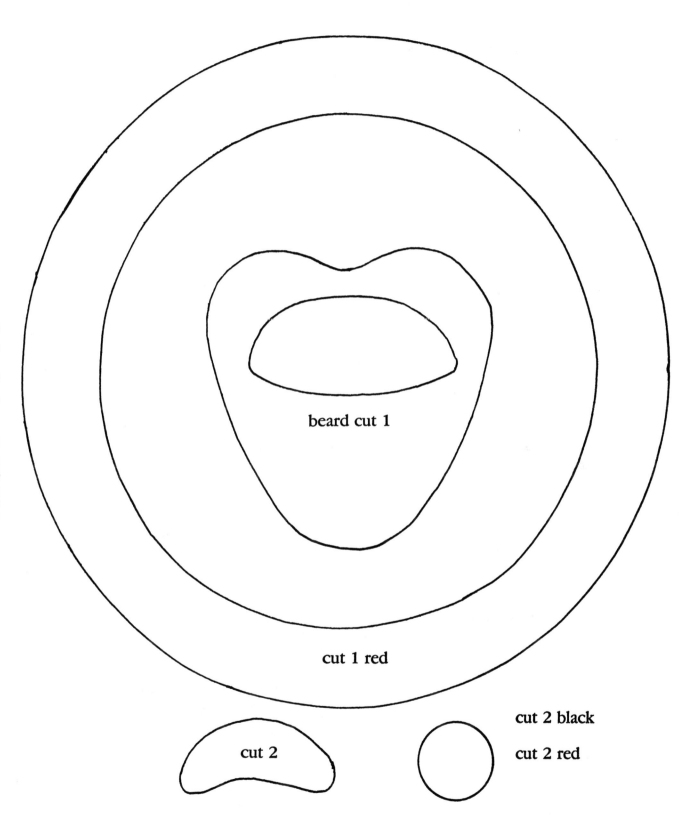

beard cut 1

cut 1 red

cut 2

cut 2 black

cut 2 red

© 1990 by Parker Publishing Company, Inc.

STYROFOAM BALL SNOWMAN

Objectives: • Fine motor control
• Listening and following directions

Supplies: Styrofoam balls, 1″ size or larger
Scissors
Paper punch
Glue
Toothpicks

Materials: Construction paper, black, 2″ × 4½″
Felt pieces, variety of colors, 2¼″ × 6½″ for the small balls (if using larger balls, increase size accordingly)
Pattern for feet
Thread
Yarn, small pieces, to match or contrast with felt colors

Directions:

1. Show a sample; then distribute materials.

2. Put two styrofoam balls together by inserting a toothpick between them.

3. Fold the black paper in half and trace the pattern for the feet with the straight side of the pattern on the fold.

4. Cut out the feet and glue together.

5. Glue the feet to one of the balls. Set aside to dry.

6. Cut a 1″ strip from the long side of the felt to make a scarf.

7. Shape the scarf by cutting a curved piece from each side, leaving the middle section about 3/8″ to 1/2″ wide.

8. Using the rest of the felt strip, turn up about 1/4″ on one long side and glue just enough to hold in position, but not enough to make it look stiff.

9. Lap the ends of the felt-strip about 1/4″ and glue. Let dry.

10. Using a needle and thread, run a basting stitch about 1/2″ to 3/4″ from the other long side of the hat and draw up to form a topknot.

11. Tie a piece of yarn around the topknot to trim it.

12. Using a paper punch, cut six dots from black paper. Glue three dots onto the bottom ball for buttons. Glue the others on the top ball for eyes and mouth.

13. Wrap the scarf around the space between the balls and tie it.

14. Place the hat on the head and, if desired, glue it in place.

SNOWMAN

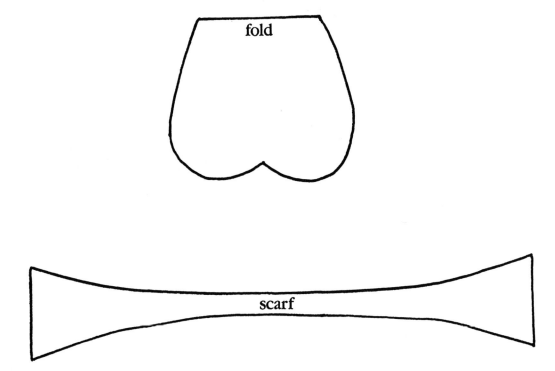

fold

scarf

━━━━━ THREE-DIMENSIONAL ORNAMENTS ━━━━━

Objectives: • Observation of change in form
• Following directions
• Seeing the need for accuracy

Supplies: Pencils
Scissors
Small paper punch or large needle
Crayons, colored pencils, or felt-tip pens

Materials: Construction or other firm paper, size and color according to project
Yarn or thread for hanging

Directions:

1. Distribute supplies and materials according to need.

2. Trace and cut out the pieces for the ornament. If ornaments are to be decorated, do that now with whichever medium you have chosen.

3. Using a punch or needle, make a hole for the hanger.

4. To assemble, begin with the solid center piece and add the other rings by bending each piece slightly so the notches will fit into each other at the top and the bottom. Add yarn or thread to hang.

5. These ornaments can be folded flat when they are not in use.

THREE-DIMENSIONAL ORNAMENTS

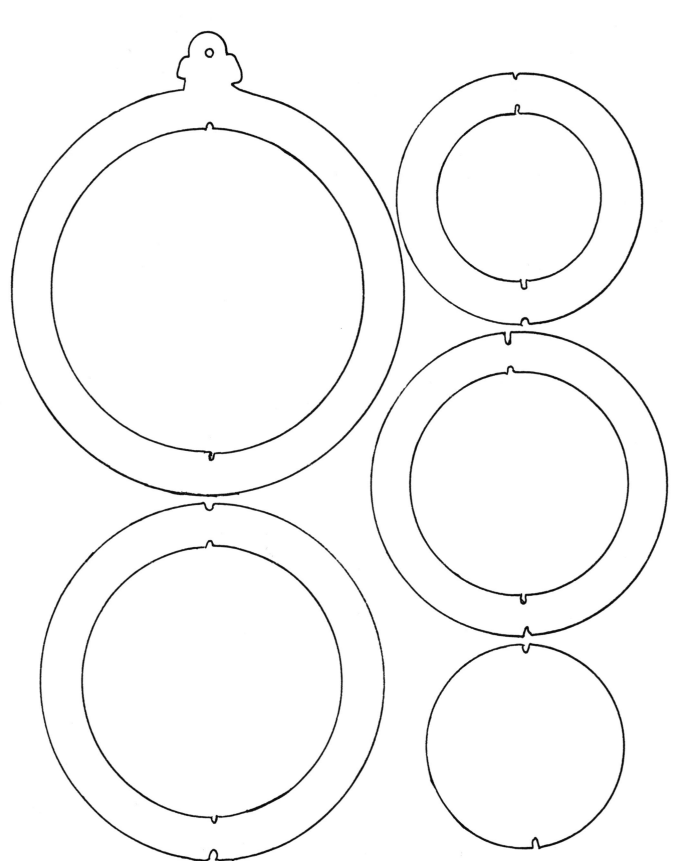

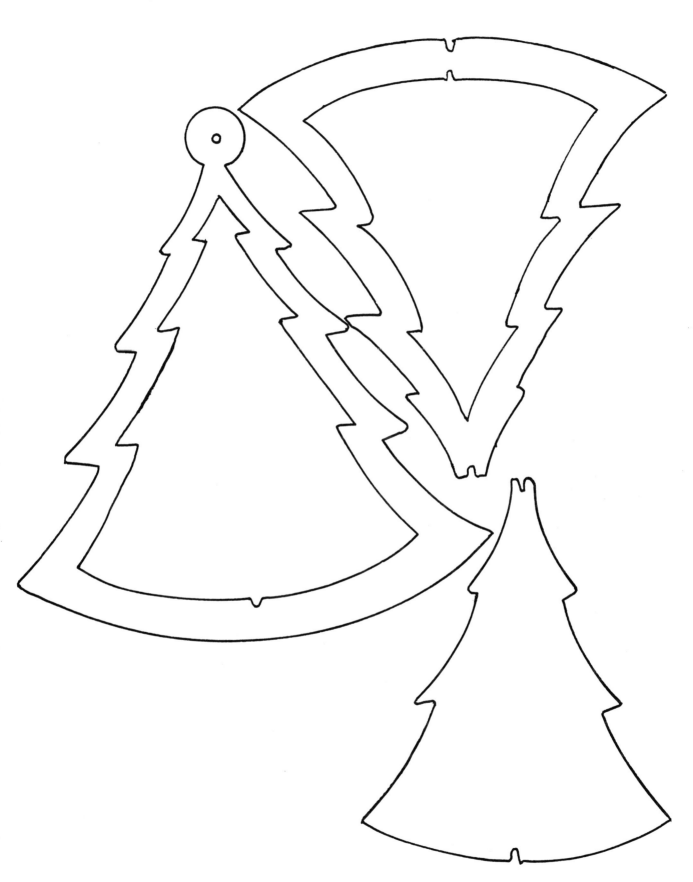

——— VALENTINE ANIMALS ———

Objectives: • Parts-to-a-whole skills
• Hand-eye coordination
• Using imagination, learning about caricature

Supplies: Pencils
Scissors
Glue

Materials: Construction or poster paper, red, pink, and black in various sizes
Heart patterns in variations of shape

Directions:

1. Talk about how paper animals might be formed from different sizes of hearts. Talk about caricatures, perhaps showing examples from newspapers or cartoons. Think about how size might suggest an animal: large—elephant, chubby—puppy or pig, long—slinky cat.

2. Distribute materials and supplies

3. Trace or cut freehand hearts in various sizes and colors.

4. Fit the hearts together in different ways to form common animal shapes.

5. When a pleasing caricature is reached, glue the pieces in place.

———— WEAVING VALENTINES ————

Objectives: • Fine motor control
  • Color blending and contrasting
  • Figure-ground discrimination
  • Following directions
  • Spacial concepts: over/under, in/out

Supplies: Scissors
  Glue
  Ruler
  Pencils

Materials: Poster paper 6″ square or larger for background, color of your choice
  Poster paper strips 1/2″ wide and as long as the widest part of the heart, color to blend or contrast
  Patterns, heart as large as background cut in half

Directions:

1. Talk about color, and demonstrate colors that blend and colors that contrast to show how the finished valentine might look.

2. Demonstrate how to weave using the vocabulary words.

3. Distribute materials and have children fold the square of paper in half.

4. Trace and cut out the heart shape. Do not unfold.

5. Measure and draw lightly 1/2″ spaces across the heart. Remember to leave about a 1/2″ margin around the entire heart.

6. Cut on the lines and unfold the heart.

7. Weave the strips of paper through the slits. Cut to fit if necessary.

8. Glue each strip in place after the weaving is finished.

Note: There are many ways in which the woven heart may be used. A message might be printed on a strip of paper and glued across the heart. The woven heart can be mounted on a larger piece of paper with space below for a message. It could be used on the cover of a folded Valentine. Another variation is to do the weaving in a traditional square and glue it to the back of a heart-shaped frame.

——— WINTER PICTURE ———

Objectives: • Shape and form recognition
• Perspective, size and depth recognition
• Sequencing and following directions
• Understanding the difference in seasons

Supplies: Scissors
Glue
Fine-tip felt pen
Chalk, white or light yellow, and blue

Materials: Construction paper, dark blue, 9″ × 12″, for background
Poster paper, white, 6″ × 12″
Poster paper, brown 1½″ or 2″ × 12″
Poster paper, small pieces in shades of gray, brown, red, black, or other colors for buildings
Patterns for roofs if children are unable to cut these shapes

Directions:

1. Show an example or describe the picture to be made; then distribute the materials.

2. Tear one edge of the brown piece of paper to look like hills or mountains.

3. Tear one side of the white piece about one third of the way (2″) from the edge.

4. Set aside the wider strip and tear a little off the straight side of the narrow strip to make it uneven.

5. Arrange the brown and two white strips of paper on the background to divide into areas of the landscape. Glue in place.

6. Cut squares from the small pieces of paper for the buildings.

7. Trace or cut freehand shapes for roofs. Make them big enough to cover the width of the buildings.

8. Cut out small squares and rectangles for doors and windows.

9. Assemble the parts of the buildings and glue in place.

10. Arrange the buildings on the background, with larger ones near the bottom so they will appear to be closer.

11. Glue the buildings in place.

12. Using the felt-tip pen, add leafless trees and bushes.

13. Using the chalk, add some shading to the hills or mountains, and show the light source by adding a few shadows.

WINTER PICTURE

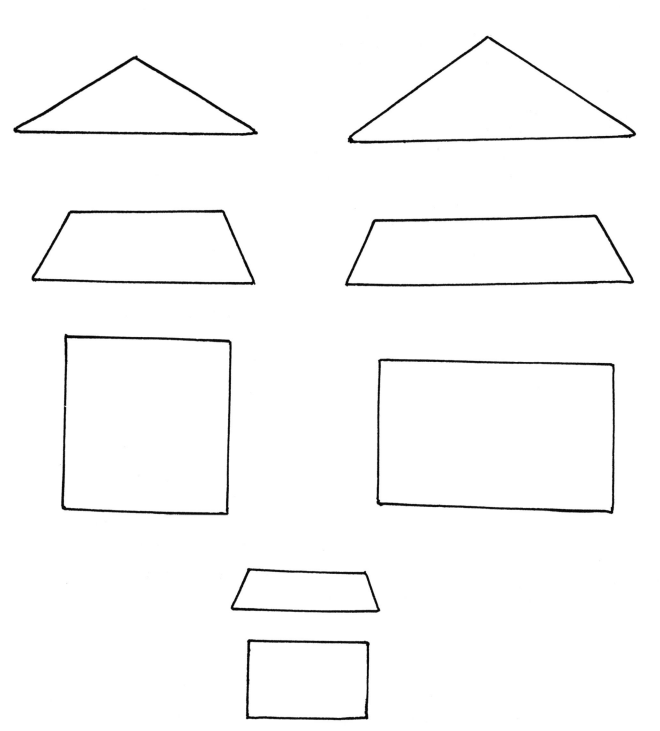

——— WINTER TREES ———

Objectives: • Vocabulary: perspective, shadows or light source
• Fine motor control
• Sequencing and following directions

Supplies: Scissors
Chalk, white
Felt-tip pen, black

Materials: Construction paper, dark blue, 9″ × 12″ for background
Poster or construction paper, light blue, 4″ × 9″
Poster paper, white, 3″ × 9″ for background hills
Poster paper, white, 4″ × 10″ for trees
Poster paper, black, 2″ × 10″ for trees
Poster paper, dark green, 6″ × 9″ for bushes

Directions:

1. Talk about vocabulary words and show examples in the picture.

2. Distribute materials and have the children tear an uneven edge on one long side of the white background piece.

2. Tear an uneven edge on one long side of the light blue paper.

4. Fit the white and light blue strips in place on the dark blue background and glue in place.

5. Tear pieces from the green paper and lay (do not glue) on the background.

6. Cut tree trunks and stub branches from the black and white paper.

7. Lay the trees and bushes on the background and adjust the positions of the bushes and trees.

8. When the perspective is accurate, glue in place.

9. Using the chalk, make tree shadows and branches on the white trees.

10. Using the felt-tip pen, add markings to the white trees, and add a few more branches.

——— WOVEN HEART BASKET ———

Objectives: • Fine motor control
  • Using a ruler
  • Following directions

Supplies: Pencils
  Rulers
  Glue

Materials: Heart pattern
  Poster paper, two colors

Directions:

1. Distribute the materials and tell children to trace the pattern on each of the colors of paper.

2. Cut out the hearts and fold on the dotted line.

3. Using the ruler and pencil, measure and mark the cutting lines.

4. Cut each heart into strips.

5. Weave the strips. Pull *gently* to straighten the strips.

6. Measure and cut a strip 1¼″ × 7½″ for a handle.

7. Glue the ends of the handle to the inside of the basket.

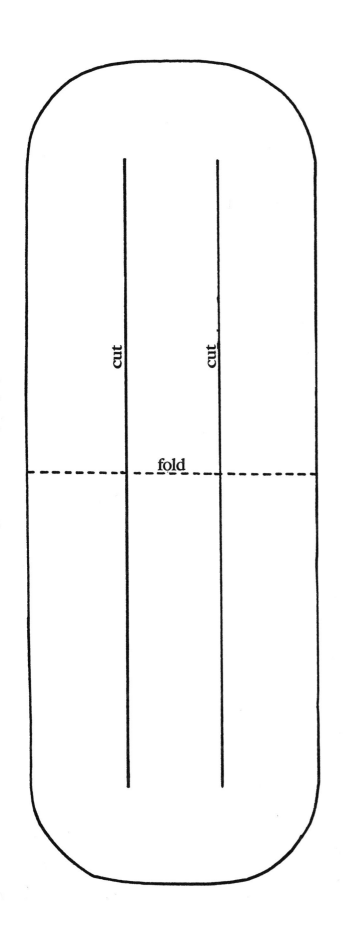

cut

cut

fold

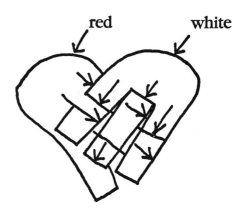

red   white

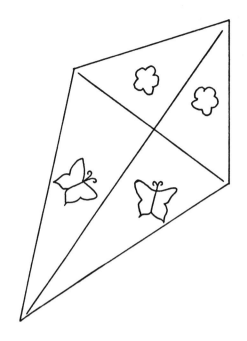

❖❖ **SPRING** ❖❖

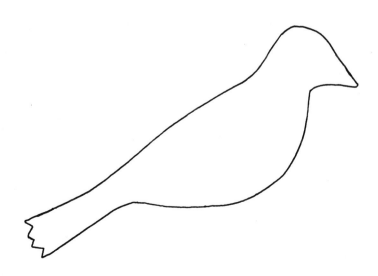

DAFFODIL

Objectives: • Sequencing oral directions
• Recognition of seasonal happenings
• Visual motor coordination

Supplies: Pencils
Scissors
Glue

Materials: Poster paper, yellow, 8″ × 9″
Poster paper, green, 4″ × 12″ for stems and leaves
Patterns or duplicated sheets

Directions:

1. Talk about things that happen in the spring, especially flowers growing. Talk about the shapes of flowers and different kinds of leaves on flowers.

2. Trace and cut out two flowers (two parts of each).

3. Along the straight edge of the rectangular piece, cut a fringe about 1/4″ in from the edge.

4. Roll the rectangle into a tube and glue the ends.

5. Fold the tabs to the center of the tube and glue to the center of the petals. Press the fringe out to form the ruffled part of the daffodil center.

6. Cut the green paper into two long strips. Use one of the strips to cut long, thin leaves.

7. Cut the other long strip of green paper into two strips. Roll the strips into spirals for the stems. Glue the ends.

8. Flatten one end of a spiral and glue it to the back of a flower. Put a stem on the other flower and glue on the leaves.

Note: One way to display the daffodils is to make a holder for them from a tall paper cup. Turn the cup over and punch a hole in the bottom. Insert the flowers. If the flowers are to be used on a bulletin board, they will look more natural if they are placed along the bottom of the board behind a strip of paper that has been cut and curled slightly to look like grass.

DAFFODIL

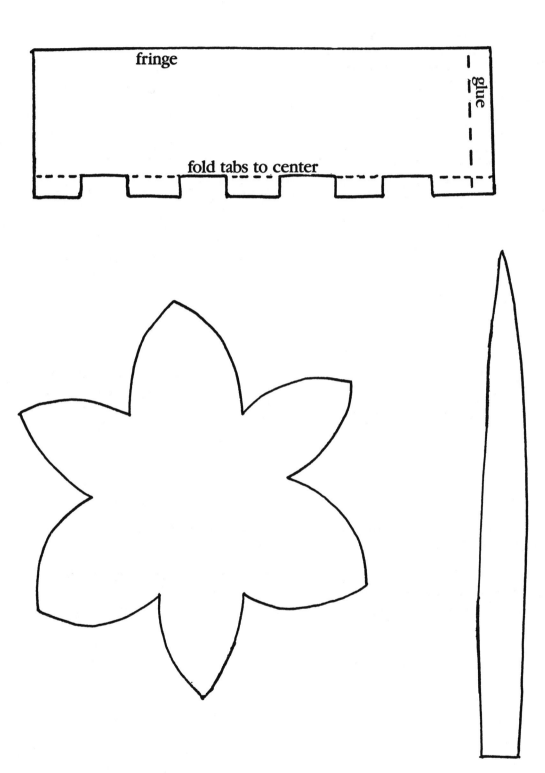

fringe

glue

fold tabs to center

─── EASTER LILY ───

Objectives: • Hand-eye coordination
• Fine motor control
• Following directions

Supplies: Pencils
Scissors
Glue

Materials: Poster or duplicating paper, white, 7″ × 7″ for each lily, three suggested
Small pieces of paper, green, 6″ long for leaves
Chenille wires, green (these are similar to pipe cleaners, but are longer and thicker)
Pattern
Construction paper for background (9″ × 12″ for one lily; larger if making more than one)

Directions:

1. Distribute supplies and materials.

2. Trace and cut out three flowers and several leaves.

3. Put glue on the tab side of the flower and glue to the inside of the flower. It may be necessary to crease it between the fingers to be sure the glue holds; then gently squeeze back to shape.

4. Make a small hole in the bottom where the chenille wire can be inserted for a stem.

5. Glue the leaves to the chenille wire.

6. Carefully curl the petals just enough to take away the stiff look of the flowers.

7. Arrange the three flowers on the background with the glued side down. Glue in place.

Note: For a different kind of picture, the flowers can be arranged in a holder cut to look like a flower pot or vase or in a woven paper basket.

For a more realistic look, the stems can be placed in a paper cup of plaster of Paris before it sets.

EASTER LILY

leaf

FISH KITE (LARGE)

Objectives: • Fine motor skills
  • Following directions
  • Using creativity in color and design

Supplies: Scissors
  Pliers
  Paper punch
  Glue
  Crayons
  Masking tape
  String
  Wire (fairly soft)
  Pencils
  Small paper clip (optional)

Materials: Kraft paper, light color or white, 22″ × 30″

Directions:

1. Fold the paper in half lengthwise.

2. Draw the fish shape, using as much of the paper as possible. Be sure to draw the mouth and tail at least 6″ to 8″ across to provide a good air passage and to make the construction easier.

3. Cut out the fish through both thicknesses of paper. Start cutting at the open side. The fold will help to hold it together until you finish cutting.

4. Glue the long sides near the edge, leaving the tail section loose and the mouth end open.

5. Color the fish with crayons on both sides. Try to position the eyes, fins, etc. as near the same place on both sides as possible.

6. Fold the edges of the mouth back about 1/2″.

7. Using the fold line as a stop, cut slits along the edge at about 1/2″ intervals.

8. Measure a piece of wire to fit the mouth edge, and leave a little extra to fasten the ends together.

9. When the wire has been fastened and shaped to an oval, fit it inside the mouth and glue the cut tabs over it to the inside.

10. Tape the inside of the mouth edge for extra strength. This can be done with several small pieces of tape.

11. Punch two holes opposite each other on the mouth edge on the flat side of the fish.

12. Cut a bridle string about 30″ long. Tie the ends through the punched holes.

13. Use a small paper clip to attach the flying line, or tie it leaving a loop so it will slide on the bridle when the kite is flown.

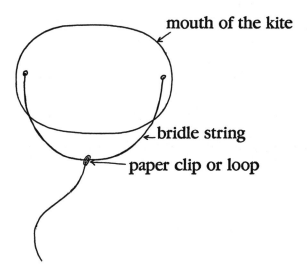

mouth of the kite

bridle string

paper clip or loop

14. If the flying line is tied to the bridle without being able to move, the kite will not twist or rise in the air properly—or a strong air current could tear the bridle out of the holes in the kite.

FLOWER BASKET

Objectives: • Organization and sequencing
  • Color coordination
  • Fine motor skills

Supplies: Scissors
  Glue
  Pencils

Materials: Small paper plates, one whole and a half of one (three plates make two baskets)
  Poster paper, small pieces of any flower colors
  Construction paper, green
  Yarn, ribbon, gift wrap, etc.
  Patterns for small flowers

Directions:

1. Trace and cut out five flowers.

2. Cut stems and leaves and glue onto the flowers. The total length should not exceed the distance across half of the paper plate. Set aside.

3. Trim the straight edge of the half plate with yarn or a strip of pretty paper.

4. Glue the flowers to the inside of the straight edge of the half plate.

5. Glue the half plate to the whole plate.

6. You may add a piece of yarn as a hanger at the top, on the back of the plate.

7. You might like to glue a little butterfly on the edge of the whole plate.

FLOWER BASKET

FOLDED BUTTERFLY

Objectives: • Visual motor integration
• Fine motor control
• Following directions

Supplies: Scissors
Pencils

Materials: Butterfly pattern
Poster paper, foil, gift wrap, or tissue paper, 8″ × 10″
Pipe cleaners or plastic-covered wire bag ties

Directions:

1. Trace and cut out the pattern.

2. Beginning at either long side, make 1/4″ fan folds all the way across, being careful to keep the folds as straight and even as possible.

3. Fasten the pipe cleaner or wire around the center while holding the folds together.

4. Spread out the wings, but do not flatten the folds.

5. Curl the ends of the pipe cleaner or wire to form the antennae.

Note: For older children or those with better motor skills, cut the pattern between the wings and use two colors of paper. Fasten the two folded pieces together with the pipe cleaner, and continue as above. The pattern may also be reduced in size for more skilled hands.

If the butterflies are to be used in potted plants, attach a second wire with which to stick the butterfly into the soil.

FOLDED BUTTERFLY

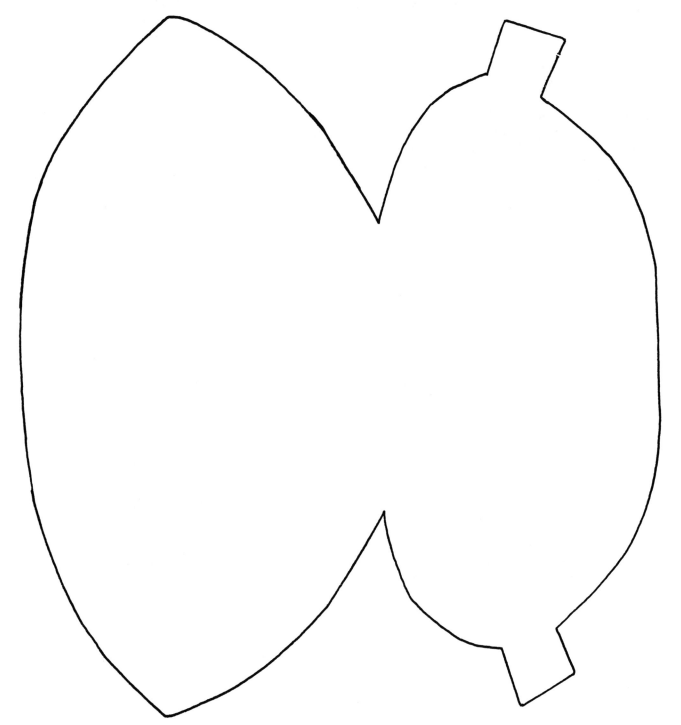

LEPRECHAUNS (TROLLS, etc.)

Objectives: • Vocabulary: leprechauns, elves, fairies, trolls, myths, legends, and other make-believe things
  • Awareness of body parts and, in particular, thumbs pointing up
  • Fine motor control

Supplies: Pencils
Scissors
Paper punch
Patterns

Materials: Poster paper, green, 4″ × 6″ for hat
Poster paper, green, 4⅝″ × 6″ to wrap tube for coat, or 6″ square to roll for body
Poster paper, black, 2¾″ × 3″ for feet
Poster paper, green, 1/2″ × 18″ for arms
Poster paper, tan, 2″ × 2″ for face
Scraps of paper, green, tan, or other colors for hands and facial features
White yarn scraps or cotton for beard and hair
Paper tubes from toilet paper or paper towels

Directions:

1. Trace and cut out all pieces using patterns. Set aside.

2. Wrap and glue paper to tube, or form a square of paper into a cylinder.

3. Glue feet to one end of tube.

4. Roll hat to fit and glue the ends where the rolled material comes together.

5. Position hat and face on tube. Glue hat to the back of the body. Do not glue face on now.

6. Add features to face. Add beard and hair. Then glue face to front of body. The top of the head should be just under the hat.

7. Fold long strips of paper in the center at a 90° angle. Then fold the paper back and forth to form spring-type arms. After folding the "spring," the two ends of the paper need to be glued or the "spring" will unfold.

8. Glue hands to arms, thumbs up.

9. Glue arms to body.

10. Add trimming to hat, buttons to coat, or any other details you would like.

LEPRECHAUNS

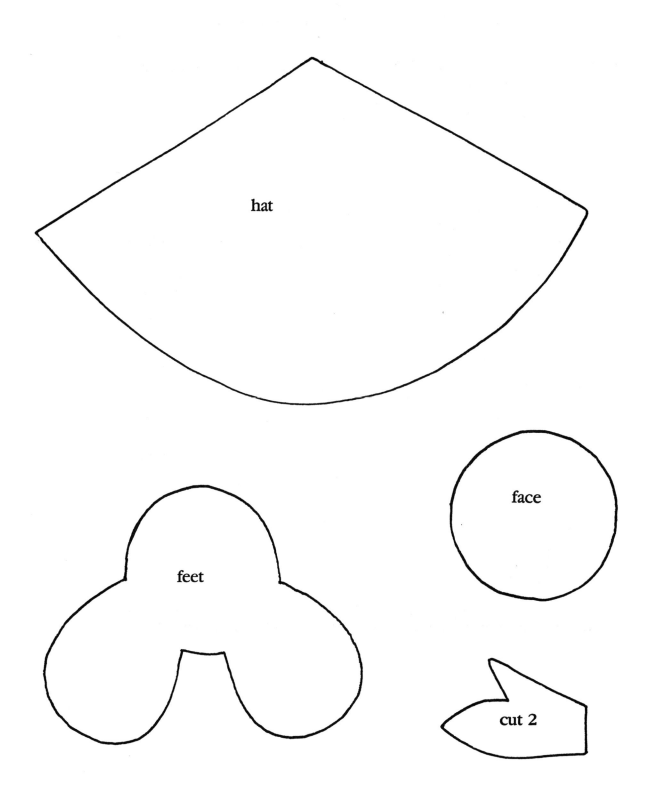

hat

face

feet

cut 2

LION AND LAMB

Objectives: • Learn about sayings: "In like a lion, out like a lamb" or the opposite
  • Importance of proportion
  • Fine motor coordination
  • Sequencing and following directions

Supplies: Scissors
  Glue
  Paper punch

Materials: Poster or construction paper for background 9″ × 12″, in blue or color to harmonize with burlap
  Burlap, two colors: white, natural, gold, tan, light green; lamb 3½″ to 4″ square; lion 3½″ × 6″ rectangle
  Scraps of poster paper in shades of brown, black, red; bits of cloth may be used instead of paper, or use scraps of burlap for the faces of the animals.

Directions:

1. Talk about the foregoing saying in relation to the weather in March. Also mention that the lion and lamb together are a symbol of peace (especially if you want to use this idea for a Christmas card).

2. Cut the square burlap into a circle by rounding off the corners. Use the rectangle as cut.

3. Fringe both the circle and the rectangle by pulling out four to six threads along each side.

4. Cut faces, ears, and lion's nose from paper, cloth, or burlap.

5. Use a paper punch to cut the eyes for both animals.

6. Arrange the features for each and glue in place.

7. Place on the background and glue.

Note: After fringing the circle, you may have to trim it to look rounded. Also note that the bottom of the lion's head should have longer fringe than the other three sides.

LION AND LAMB

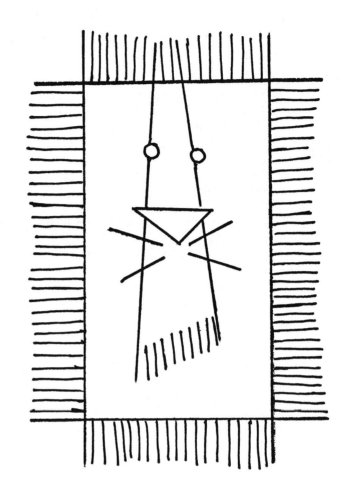

L. R. D. Publishing Company, Inc.

MOTHER'S DAY CARD

Objectives: • Color coordination
• Sequencing directions
• Visual and fine motor integration

Supplies: Scissors
Fine-tip felt pens, red, black, brown, or blue
Buttons, white or tan, two holes, 3/4″ across
Felt, small pieces in a variety of colors
Ribbon, 1/8″ to 1/4″ wide in a choice of colors
Small silk flowers in harmonizing colors
Glue

Materials: Construction paper or lightweight card stock, 4″ or 5″ wide and twice as long as the width
Patterns for hats

Directions:

1. Choose colors that will look good together for the felt, ribbon, and flower.

2. Cut out the hat shape.

3. Glue the ribbon and flower to the hat. Set this aside.

4. Fold the card in half to form a square.

5. Position the button midway from the sides and about two thirds of the way down from the top of the card.

6. Glue the button in place.

7. Using the felt-tip pens, add a pair of eyes by marking through the holes of the button. Also add eyebrows and a mouth.

8. Position the hat over the button face and glue down.

Note: With younger children or those who have difficulty with cutting, it is less frustrating if you have the hat shapes cut out ahead of time. It is hard to trace on felt, and the children may have difficulty cutting around the pattern.

MOTHER'S DAY CARD

MOTHER'S DAY CORSAGE

Objectives: • Eye-hand coordination
              • Fine motor control
              • Spatial awareness

Supplies: Pencils
          Scissors
          Glue

Materials: Pattern for back (optional)
Construction paper, green, 4″ square and 2″ square
Tissue paper in flower colors, 2″ squares (the number will vary according to how it is used)
Poster paper, white or another color of your choice, 1″ × 9″

Directions:

1. Trace and cut background from the green square.

2. Round off the 2″ square to form a circle.

3. Using a square of tissue, place the flat end of a pencil in the center and crush the tissue around the pencil.

4. Put a dot of glue on the paper at the end of the pencil.

5. Press the tissue onto the 2″ circle and pull out the pencil.

6. Repeat the preceding directions with more tissue until the circle is filled, forming the flower.

7. Glue the circle to the center of the background.

8. Fold the strip of paper and trim the ends to resemble a ribbon.

9. Write *Happy Mother's Day* on the ribbon.

10. Glue the ribbon to the back of the corsage.

MOTHER'S DAY CORSAGE

flower base

——— ORIENTAL POPPIES ———

Objectives: • Fine motor control
• Visual, hand-eye coordination
• Following directions, sequencing

Supplies: Pencils
Scissors
Glue
Chenille wire, green if possible
Florist tape (optional)

Materials: Tissue paper, orange
Crepe paper, green and black
Construction paper, green for leaves
Patterns

Directions:

1. Distribute supplies and materials. If using green wires, only small pieces of green crepe paper are needed. If using florist tape, no green crepe paper is needed.

2. Cut the tissue paper in strips 4½″ to 5″ wide.

3. Fold the tissue paper so that it ends up as a 3″-wide piece.

4. Trace the petal pattern on the top of the folded paper and cut out several petals at one time. There must be a total of fifteen or sixteen petals. Set aside.

5. Using a piece of black crepe paper about 3″ square, cut one side in a fringe for the center of the flower.

6. Roll the fringed paper and bend an end of the wire to hold it.

7. Place the petals around the center of the flower and pinch in the bottom. If necessary, add a tiny drop of glue occasionally to keep the petals from sliding off or down the stem.

8. When all the petals are in place, if you have used green wire, use a small piece of green paper or florist tape to the cover the bottom of the flower. If you have not used green wire, cover the bottom of the flower, and then cover the stem with the florist tape or a 1/2″ strip of green crepe paper with a drop of glue on the starting end (where the strip of paper is attached—before wrapping the

stem). Whatever you use to wrap the stem, it must be done on a diagonal or it will bunch up and will not come out smooth.

9. Add leaves near the bottom of the stem.

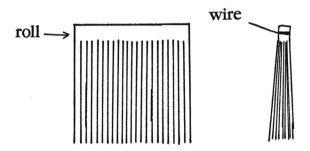

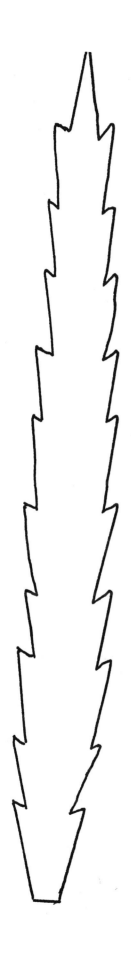

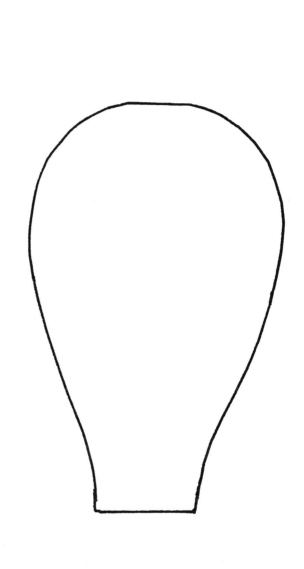

———— PAPER STRIP BIRDS ————

Objectives: • Fine motor control
              • Following directions
              • Awareness of nature created in fantasy

Supplies: Stapler
              Paper clips

Materials: Poster or construction paper, 1″ × 12″ strips in a variety of colors

Directions:

1. Discuss with the children how we fantasize about familiar objects in nature by using different colors and shapes that suggest what we are thinking about.

2. Distribute four strips of paper to each child.

3. Place the ends of three strips together. Fasten with a paper clip about 1″ from the end.

4. Add the last strip on top, extending it about 5″ beyond the ends of the other three strips.

5. Staple the four strips together, about 1/2″ from the end of the three strips. Remove paper clip.

6. Holding the strips together about 2″ from the other end of the top strip (now shorter than the rest), loosen the strips so there is about 1/2″ to 3/4″ space between them. Staple together about 2″ from the end of the top strip.

7. On the end stapled first, curl the top strip between the thumb and first finger. This forms the bird's head.

8. Crease the other three strips to form the beak.

9. Curl the strips on the other end, up and down, to form the tail feather.

Note: You can use glue or paste rather than a stapler, in which case you must hold the pieces in place until the glue dries. A variation is to glue the strips evenly on one end, then space the strips to form a head, and glue in place. Form the body by spacing the strips and gluing again; then curl the tail. This will result in a larger tail. Also, by holding the strips and gluing them together below the staple so that the strips do not separate into the bird's body, you can have a bird with a long neck. By using different color combinations, the birds can become quite exotic.

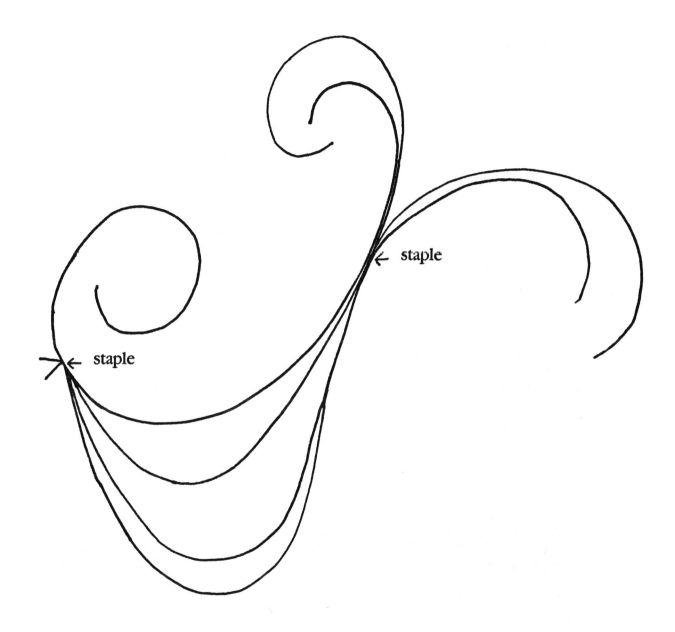

staple

staple

———— ROBIN ————

Objectives: • Seasonal changes
• Fine motor control
• Eye-hand coordination

Supplies: Scissors
Pencils
Glue

Materials: Poster or construction paper, brown, 5″ × 8″
Poster paper, copper or deep orange, 3″ × 4½″
Patterns

Directions:

1. Trace and cut bird and two wings from brown paper.

2. Trace and cut two breasts from copper paper.

3. Glue the copper-colored pieces on each side of the bird, the pointed end toward the tail.

4. Fold down the tab on the wings and glue one to each side near the shoulder of the bird. Be sure the feather side of the wing is down.

5. A small black dot may be added for an eye, if desired.

ROBIN

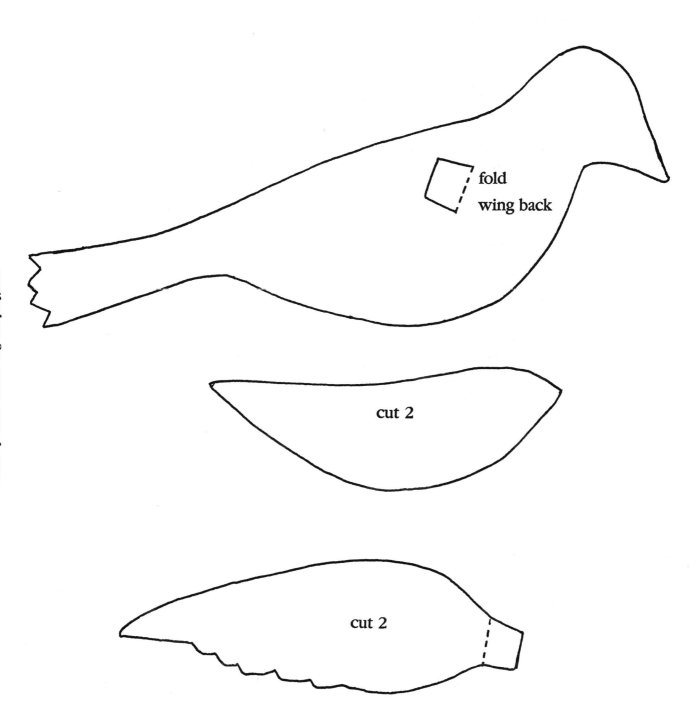

fold
wing back

cut 2

cut 2

─────── TISSUE PAPER KITE (SMALL) ───────

Objectives: • Sequencing directions
• Fine motor control
• Kite safety

Supplies: Scissors
Glue

Materials: Tissue paper, any color, 9″ × 12″
Small scraps of poster paper
Sticks (from matchstick blinds or fireworks sticks) one 11″, one 6″ long
Lightweight string 18″ long

Directions:

1. Talk about kite safety.

2. Fold tissue in half lengthwise.

3. Fold tissue about a third of the way from one end.

4. Unfold and apply a fine line of glue along the lengthwise fold about 1/2″ from each end.

5. Place the long stick on the glue and press down to secure in place.

6. Repeat the preceding directions on the short fold.

7. Fold the top corners to the center and glue over the end of the long stick.

8. Fold the bottom sides on a diagonal from the center to the end of the short stick.

9. Glue the edges using as little glue as possible.

10. Glue one end of the string to the narrow end of the kite.

11. At intervals along the string, glue pieces of paper for the tail.

12. Using more scraps of paper, cut and glue decorations on the kite.

Note: These are not really meant to fly, but they will if another piece of string is glued where the sticks cross over each other. They really are too small and fragile for outdoor kites.

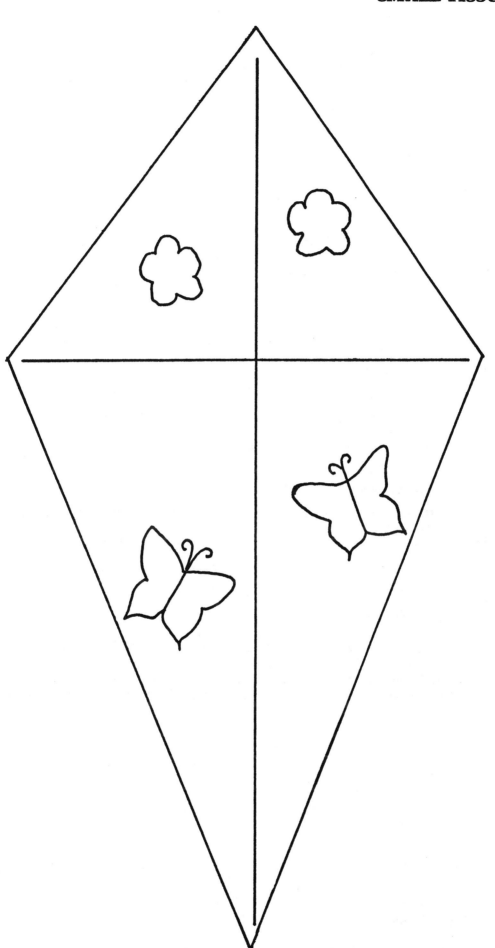

——— TISSUE TULIP ———

Objectives: • Reinforcement of seasonal changes
• Sequencing and organization
• Shapes and proportion

Supplies: Scissors
Glue

Materials: Manila or light blue poster or construction paper for the background
Poster paper, green, half sheet of 9″ × 12″ paper
Tissue paper, variety of colors, 2″ squares
Leaf pattern (optional)

Directions:

1. Using three or four tissue squares for each tulip, fold two squares in half diagonally. Set aside.

2. Fold the third square diagonally; then fold diagonally again.

3. To form each flower, place the two larger triangles with the open side of one along the folded side of the other; then turn up the pointed end about 1/2″ or 3/4″.

4. Using just a dab of glue, fasten these two pieces together.

5. Place the smaller triangle behind the petals formed in step 2 with the point up. Glue in place. Set aside.

6. Cut thin stems, about 1/4″ wide and of various lengths from 3″ to 5″.

7. Cut or trace and cut out leaves, two for each flower.

8. Glue the stem to the back of the tulip and the leaves at the very bottom of the stem.

9. Arrange three or four tulips on the background and glue in place.

Note: If you would like a softer color, use two pieces of tissue in different colors such as pink and purple or red, or try yellow and orange.

TISSUE TULIP

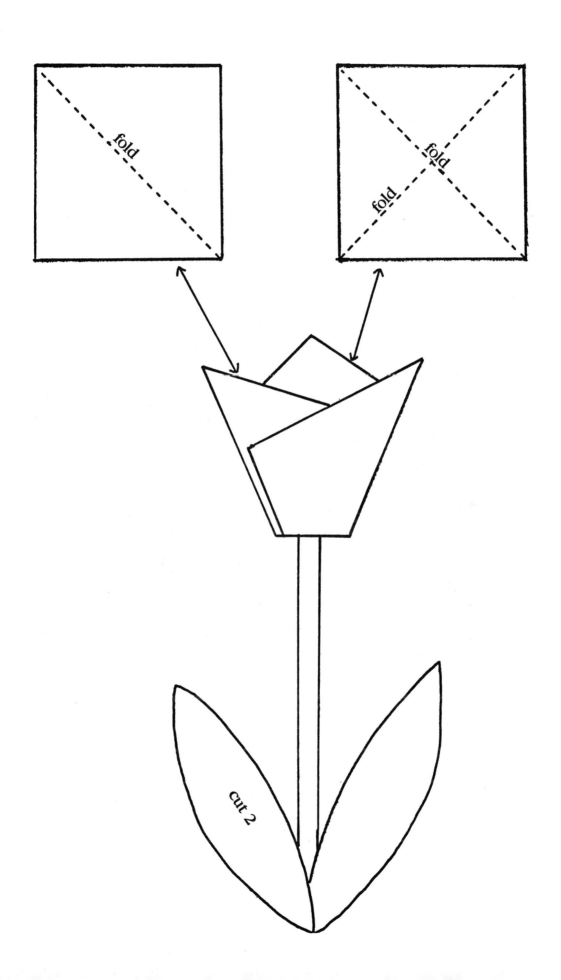

fold

fold

fold

fold

cut 2

© 1990 by Parker Publishing Company, Inc.